AMERICAN ESSAYS IN LITURGY

Feminist Liturgy

AMERICAN ESSAYS IN LITURGY

Series Editor, Edward Foley

Feminist Liturgy
A Matter of Justice

Janet R. Walton

A Liturgical Press Book

THE LITURGICAL PRESS
Collegeville, Minnesota

The author gratefully acknowledges the use of copyrighted texts on pp. 55, 56, 60, and 67 in this book:

"Greeting: New Year's Eve, 1937" by May Sarton, from *Selected Poems of May Sarton* by Serena Sue Hilsinger and Lois Byrnes, editors. Copyright © 1978 by May Sarton. Reprinted by permission of W. W. Norton & Company, Inc.

Reprinted from *When Madness Comes Home: Help and Hope for the Families of the Mentally Ill* by Victoria Secunda. Copyright © 1977 by Victoria Secunda. Published by Hyperion.

Excerpt, as submitted, from "Kaddish" from *Collected Poems, 1947–1980* by Allen Ginsberg. Copyright renewed. Reprinted by permission of Harper-Collins Publishers, Inc. For additional territory, please contact Penguin Books Limited, 27 Wrights Lane, London W8 5TZ England.

"Is That All There Is?" by Jerry Leiber, Mike Stoller © 1966 (renewed) Jerry Leiber Music, Mike Stoller Music. All rights reserved. Used by permission.

Scripture selections unless otherwise noted are taken from the New Revised Standard Version Bible, © 1989 by the Division of Christian Education of the National Council of Churches of Christ in the U.S.A. Used by permission. All rights reserved.

1   2   3   4   5   6   7   8   9

Library of Congress Cataloging-in-Publication Data

Walton, Janet Roland.
    Feminist liturgy : a matter of justice / Janet R. Walton.
        p.   cm. — (American essays in liturgy)
    Includes bibliographical references.
    ISBN 0-8146-2596-7 (alk. paper)
    1. Catholic Church—Liturgy.   2. Feminist theology.   3. Catholic women—Religious life.   I. Title.   II. Series: American essays in liturgy (Collegeville, Minn.)
BX1970.W2557   2000
264'.02'0082—dc21   99-43619
                                             CIP

To my nieces and nephews
with the hope that feminist liturgies
will be a regular part of their lives:
Elizabeth, Katharine, Sarah, Brendan, Robby,
Mark, Liz, Spencer, Mary Beth, Chris, Andrew, and Emily

Contents

Acknowledgments

This book is the result of many years of restlessness, determination, experimentation, and hope. It represents my longing for liturgies that are more expressive of what we know about God and ourselves, a knowledge that changes and grows, for liturgies that are more connected to the choices we make daily, risk-taking as a mandate of liturgical action, for liturgies that extend what is holy to what is not yet imagined. Many people share this same dream and the work to achieve it.

For seventeen years I have been a member of the Women's Liturgy Group in New York City. We meet once a month to imagine and to do feminist liturgy. Each member contributed in varied ways to the ideas expressed here. For seventeen years also, I have been a member of the Union Theological Seminary community where students, faculty, staff, and administrators try ways of embodying what we are learning in the classroom and in our lives. It is rigorous, collective work.

While writing this book I turned to people from these groups to read sections of it. I am grateful to Mary Ragan, Beverly Coyle, Claire S. Derway, Annette Covatta, Jeanne Audrey Powers, Ginger Worden, Kosuke Koyama, Rosemary Keller, Delores Williams, Ana-Maria Diaz Stevens, and Susan Blain for their help and suggestions. I am also indebted to Union students Yuki Yamamoto and Eileen Crowley-Horak for their research and technical assistance. They gathered much more than I asked. There are others, too. Marjorie Procter-Smith reminded me of some important omissions. Margaret Moers Wenig provided the example about mental illness and Beryl Ingram, the example about sexual abuse. Ed Foley extended the deadlines generously when I realized that the writing was more complicated than I anticipated.

Family members and friends provided constant presence and encouragement. Bob Johnson edited the manuscript carefully and quickly. Dick Vosko not only pointed out missing details but also the need to get this book done, now. Anne E. Patrick critiqued and edited several drafts. The Sisters of the Holy Names gave me space and support to experiment with ideas. The Luce Foundation and Union Theological Seminary made it possible to have time off from regular teaching to work on this manuscript. Finally, I want to thank Ann Patrick Ware. She not only read every word more than once, offering insight, affirmation, and concrete suggestions, but much more. She is a treasured friend and partner in realizing this dream. One day, after church seventeen years ago, Ann Pat Ware and I decided to use constructively the disappointment and anger we felt regularly in church. We gathered some friends, Eileen King, Sarah Ryan, Cindy Derway, and Anne McGlinchey, to imagine what we could do differently. This Women's Liturgy Group, expanded and ever changing, continues to this day; it is part of a widespread movement to provide for ourselves what our institutions would not. And it is marvelous. We await a time to share with the churches and synagogues what we have learned. This book is one step toward that conversation.

Introduction

"Feminist liturgy? Impossible," says my Uncle Clarence.[1] "Feminism is a contemporary critique of culture focused on women's rights. Liturgy is a timeless, sacred blessing of God. Feminist liturgy? It's a contradiction in terms. Feminism is too exclusive, limited, and political."

Conversations with my uncle often begin with provocative statements. Since we respect each other, these conversations rarely stop at a defensive juncture. Instead we keep talking until we begin to hear what each other is saying. In the end we still may not agree, but we always learn something and we move to another level of appreciation of each other's perspectives.

I have written this book to encourage conversation among those who, like my uncle, are skeptical of efforts to "genderize liturgy" or who have never known or imagined an experience of authentic worship described as feminist liturgy. Questions about feminist liturgy abound. Hunches, doubts, and enthusiasm abound, too. This book attempts to respond to questions, clarify hunches, alleviate doubts, and encourage many more people, including my uncle, to contribute to the development of feminist liturgies.

Liturgies typically described as "feminist" began to emerge in the late 1960s when women and some men realized that what they were experiencing in the liturgies of churches and synagogues was not

---

[1] As the former president of a Catholic university and a scholar and teacher of business, Clarence Walton enjoys a good argument. Regularly we challenge each other to uphold our points of view on a wide spectrum of topics. Feminism is one of them.

11

only not "enough," but, in fact, was not "true."[2] A liturgical process that centers on an encounter, an engaged, embodied dialogue with God, cannot be true when females are left out of the dialogue, as Marjorie Procter-Smith points out. Traditional liturgical patterns have been shaped by patriarchal values, where males, particularly privileged white males, are accorded power and authority while everyone else, including all females, are without status or identity. As a result, interpretations of texts, symbols, and metaphors, the "stuff" of liturgical experiences, have been limited and distorted. We asked ourselves what would be true to our experience of what is sacred. Early on, we recognized that an answer would best be found by doing rather than talking or wishing. Feminist liturgies began when people got together to discover how to use symbols, texts, and forms that expressed relationships with God, one another, and our created world more accurately and more authentically. The quest is a matter of justice.

Feminist liturgy is not esoteric or "weird" nor only for women. On the contrary, it is ordinary, organic[3] and for everyone. Feminist liturgy expresses covenanted relationships; it renews connections between everyday human experiences and the active presence of God, which may, at times, feel like God's absence. The primary goal of feminist liturgy is to draw together *all* aspects of our relationships in ritual contexts that promote truth-telling. A community gathers to embody an encounter with God, to remember stories, particularly untold stories, and to imagine each person's place in them: stories of God, humans and other-kind in relation to each other, where *each* one's story makes a difference in what every other person understands. Though feminist liturgy got its momentum in large part from women and though it initially addressed much of what women noticed was not true for them in institutional liturgies, feminist liturgy is ultimately not just for women, but for all people. It is a search for ways to pray with delight rather than disappointment, with expectation rather than dread, with thanks rather than fear, connecting the worship of God with justice.

[2] Marjorie Procter-Smith develops this "fundamental truth question" in *In Her Own Rite: Constructing Feminist Liturgical Tradition* (Nashville: Abingdon Press, 1990) 13–35.

[3] Theologian Delores Williams, a colleague at Union Theological Seminary, applies the term "organic" to theology that grows out of persons' lives. It is equally apt to describe feminist liturgy.

The story of feminist liturgy began in the midst of a broad human quest for justice in the latter part of the twentieth century. The civil rights movement and the anti-Vietnam War movement added momentum for women's struggle for justice. Within this ferment women addressed the limits placed on them in secular and religious institutions as well. Feminist liturgies developed as one of a number of attempts to discover and claim a more truthful telling and embodying of the myths that shape our religious consciousness.

This book treats four aspects of feminist liturgies: the historical context in which they developed; the tasks and principles that guide them; the possibilities they offer; and, applications to institutional liturgies.[4] The story of feminist liturgy is in its early stages of development. What follows is only a partial account. I offer it to encourage both discussion and action so that our liturgies will be "true" for all of us, or at least in this imperfect world, for more of us.

---

[4] The origins of feminist liturgy in this essay are drawn from women's history because that is where feminist liturgy began. As women and some men identified the interconnection of oppressions with power, authority, dominance of all sorts, the history spreads more widely to include all expressions of discrimination.

1 Feminist Liturgy: Its Historical Context

When historians look back at the twentieth century from a longer vantage point than this one, they will point out with more assurance the threads of pivotal secular and religious movements that are woven into the history of feminist liturgy. From this vantage I can only offer a tentative sketch of the factors that have contributed to this important development in the history of religions. The need for feminist liturgy is rooted deeply and widely. No one date can document its beginning. It developed gradually from a confluence of historical, political, secular, and religious awarenesses. The struggles of early twentieth-century movements on behalf of women, as well as other historical changes provided a foundation for feminist liturgy.

Persistent efforts in churches and synagogues to acknowledge the leadership of women and other traditionally marginalized people also influenced its growth. Feminist liturgies emerged from varied communal and individual attempts to right what was wrong and make visible what had been hidden about God and about ourselves. Since there are readily available resources about these historical influences,[1] I offer here a few brief examples, enough to suggest the historical and cultural connections with the commitments and principles of feminist liturgy. I have chosen three quite different examples from United States history: women's participation in the labor force during World War II, the social protest movements of the 1960s, and the influential phase of the women's movement as ex-

[1] Howard Zinn, *The Twentieth Century: A People's History of the United States* (New York: HarperPerennial, 1998); Susan Hill Lindley, *You have stept out of your place* (Louisville: Westminster/John Knox, 1996).

pressed in *The Feminine Mystique* by Betty Friedan.[2] I conclude with pertinent history in the churches and synagogues.

I want to emphasize that the story of feminist liturgy has been significantly affected by differences among us and especially the impact of varied experiences of race/ethnicity, class, and sexual orientation. The specifics of our histories matter in ways we have not always recognized. Our differences divide us one from another and, at times, even alienate us. No person's story is quite like any other's, and no story includes all of us. Generalizations do not *always* apply. The development of feminist liturgy reflects the struggles and challenges of these differences.

A. Women's Participation in the Labor Force during and after World War II

When men were summoned into the war, women were called upon to fill their jobs. Early on, employers tried in vain to find male workers, including unemployed men and those ineligible for the draft, but eventually the number of vacancies and wartime needs pressed them to open jobs to women. Single women, and even more significantly, married women and women over thirty-five, responded and joined the work force. Between 1940 and 1945 six million women (an increase of 50 percent) took jobs outside their homes.[3]

Some women, who had already been employed, changed to "men's jobs," for example, from beautician to switchman, from designer of perfume bottles to precision toolmaker.[4] Others worked in factories and clerical positions in offices. Still others moved into jobs as engineers, statisticians, journalists, doctors, and lawyers.[5] Teresa Amott and Julie Matthaei point out that women from all racial/ethnic backgrounds "moved up a rung on the job ladder."[6] African American women who had been in private domestic work moved to

[2] Since this book is intended to be brief, I have limited the historical section to U.S. history. Many other global influences also could be cited.

[3] William H. Chafe, *The American Woman: Her Changing Social, Economic, and Political Role, 1920–1970* (New York: Oxford University Press, 1972) 135.

[4] Chafe, 137.

[5] Chafe, 135–50.

[6] Teresa L. Amott and Julie A. Matthaei, *Race, Gender and Work: A Multicultural Economic History of Women in the United States* (Boston: South End Press, 1991) 131.

jobs in factories and offices.[7] Chinese American women left the ghettos of Chinatown for positions in the civil service, factories, and professional fields.[8] Latinas made shifts from agriculture to clerical, professional, and defense jobs. Some Native American women found employment in the defense industries since their migration to the cities only began during the war. So significant was the effect of these changes in job opportunities that The Women's Bureau (a federal agency concerned with the development of women's participation in society) called the increase in female employment during the war years "one of the most fundamental social and economic changes in our time."[9]

The effects of this shift in employment patterns were not only economic and social, but personal as well. Women who had presumed they would always be full-time mothers and wives discovered the satisfactions of work: the power of self-reliance, the enjoyment of being paid for what they did, and, particularly significant for the work involved in feminist liturgies, the importance of supporting each other, and developing solidarity in the face of changes of all kinds. It was an experience of the company of women:

> When I first went out on the floor my presence was a constant harassment to the older women in my unit. I didn't know what to do, had to ask a lot of questions, filed incorrectly. . . . "Don't feel bad," one or another would say at a particularly stupid error. "We were all new once. We've all been through it. Don't worry. You'll catch on."[10]

This story of change, satisfaction, and new consciousness did not affect all women equally or at the same time. Many black women, already in the labor force primarily as domestic (70 percent) and agricultural (20 percent) workers, were not recruited until employers had no other options.[11] "The great employment wave withered to a trickle when it came to black workers in general and black women in particular," Paula Giddings reports.[12]

[7] Amott and Matthaei, 173.

[8] Amott and Matthaei, 209.

[9] Chafe, 148–49.

[10] Eleanor Langer, *Women at Work* as cited in Carol Hymowitz and Michaele Weissman, *A History of Women in America* (New York: Bantam Books, 1978) 319.

[11] Chafe, 142.

[12] Paula Giddings, *When and Where I Enter: The Impact of Black Women on Race and Sex in America* (New York: Bantam Books, 1984) 235.

Black women did not get employment early in the war effort for a variety of reasons: employers did not want to hire blacks, white women did not want to work with non-whites, and in some situations, white women feared the loss of their domestic help if black women were hired in jobs outside homes.[13] When blacks were hired, men were given priority and women were enlisted for jobs no one else wanted. Giddings observes that black women did "the dirtiest and most taxing jobs . . . as grinders in the steel mills and in the defense industries in custodial positions."[14]

Black women did not accept this degradation without speaking. According to Giddings, "Nearly one-quarter of all complaints to the Federal Employment Practices Commission between July 1943 and December 1944 were brought by black women."[15] Their insistence on fairness bore fruit. Between 1940 and 1944 more black women had jobs in semiprofessional occupations than as domestics, and some had gained significant leadership positions in the armed services.[16] Such was the gain, that "from a median income that was 38 percent that of white women and 51 percent that of black men in 1939, they would enjoy the greatest percentage increase of a race or sex group in the subsequent decades."[17]

The struggles of Japanese American women share some similarities with those of African American women. Most also had worked as domestics before the war. Once released from relocation camps, they first tended to take the readily available jobs in domestic service. However, by 1950 there were more Japanese American women in secretarial jobs, factory jobs or sales than in domestic labor.[18]

Latinas made similar shifts from agriculture to clerical, professional, and service jobs, especially in the wake of the war. Women who had been working in the fields moved to garment factories and to white-collar work.[19] As white women took jobs in defense industries, Latinas assumed their jobs making clothing. Altagracia Ortiz

[13] Giddings, 237.

[14] Giddings, 237.

[15] Giddings, 237–38.

[16] Giddings, 238.

[17] Giddings, 238.

[18] As cited by Valerie Matsumoto, "Japanese American Women During World War II" in *Unequal Sisters: A Multicultural Reader in U.S. Women's History*, ed. Vicki L. Ruiz and Ellen Carol DuBois (New York: Routledge, 1994) 445.

[19] Amott and Matthaei, 50, 80.

shows that Puerto Rican women were especially coveted for their expert abilities as needleworkers.[20] Though detailed information is scarce it is clear that Latinas, legal and undocumented, struggled and secured better job opportunities during the war and post-war years.

Native women gained less professionally than any other women from wartime economy.[21] Very limited numbers of Native American women were employed in defense industries or clerical positions for most had not yet moved from reservations into urban areas.

Women for whom work opportunities changed soon found that social norms, child care options, spousal expectations, and priorities given to men as the "bread winners," did not shift so quickly. Married women, according to prevailing norms, were, first and foremost, wives and mothers. When they worked, whether for economic survival or their own professional satisfaction, they were viewed by many to have jeopardized the development of children and the comfort of their husbands. Women had to prove they could "do it all."

In addition, though women had done "men's work" during the war, the jobs available to women afterwards were often "female" jobs, which carried less prestige and power than men's. Women were expected to be secretaries rather than presidents, teachers rather than principals, nurses rather than doctors, clerks rather than managers. Even in those few places where men and women had equivalent positions, women received less pay and had to be better prepared than men for the same jobs. With all these restrictions and even though many times their contributions were not taken seriously, women still persisted in public work. Some women needed the income to keep their families out of poverty, or to provide middle-class advantages for them.[22] Others wanted the option to choose work outside their homes.

For African Americans, women as well as men, race played a role in their employment options after the war. When whites returned to the job market blacks were among the first to be fired or forced down the job ladder.[23] Such was the severity of this situation that Maya Angelou commented: "We lived through a major war. The question in the ghettos [is], Can we make it though a minor peace?"[24] Black women

[20] Altagracia Ortiz, ed., *Puerto Rican Women and Work: Bridges in Transnational Labor* (Philadelphia: Temple University Press, 1996) 59.

[21] Amott and Matthaei, 50.

[22] Hymowitz and Weissman, 314.

[23] Amott and Matthaei, 320.

[24] Maya Angelou as cited in Amott and Matthaei, 173.

faced double discrimination, but as Paula Giddings testifies, even with "two steps forward and one step back," their income increased "more than any race or sex group in the subsequent decades."[25]

Work for women during the war certainly did not erase the persistence of the exploitation of women, nor did it eradicate the perception of women's inferior social status. But doors were opened that would never be shut again. Some racial/ethnic women who had left household service employment and agriculture during the war were able to stay in industry and in white-collar jobs. A long, difficult journey to insure a choice for more racial/ethnic women had begun. Married women, as well as those over thirty-five, who had joined the work force remained employed outside their homes. No doubt many would be treated like "girls" and "kids," but their participation in public work over time would lead to significant changes in attitudes toward women, "women's work" and the responsibilities of both men and women for the care of home and children.

Public work for a broader spectrum of women, though different for each woman and accompanied by particular problems, exposed the reality of the untapped potential of many women. Men and women experienced many women's capacities to contribute differently to society. What the war had required, women now desired. There was no turning back.

Whereas it would be years before there was evidence of a similar momentum to evaluate women's roles within most religious institutions, the impact of employment experiences certainly spread beyond work and stirred critical reflection about women's place in society. Why should women return to what they had done before? Why should they be invisible partners to men? Why don't women have equal participation in decisions at home and at work? What does it mean to stand in solidarity with women, of diverse backgrounds?

What had been presented historically as unchallenged "universal truths" about gender, race, ethnic, and class differences was now seen more accurately as interpretations framed by a patriarchal bias. Privileged, white male patterns of power and authority had defined the capacities of everyone else, including all women. As this paradigm was questioned and monolithic "truths" began to unravel, the seeds of feminist liturgy were planted. Such challenges to unilateral power dominated the decade of the 1960s.

[25] Giddings, 238.

B. The Social Protest Movements of the 1960s

"We shall pay any price, bear any burden, meet any hardship, support any friend, oppose any foe, in order to assure the survival and the success of liberty."[26] With these words in his 1961 inaugural address, John F. Kennedy made a commitment to the people of the United States to place freedom at the heart of his political agenda. No one, least of all the President, expected quick or easy justice, but he made a public commitment to work toward it. His words empowered others. The 1960s were a time of hope, a time to correct attitudes and make new policies. Though the struggles to challenge biased privileges were not new, Kennedy added his presidential power and his charisma to create a fresh momentum to press on in pursuit of justice for every person.

The decade of the 1960s was marked by protests for human rights and against U.S. participation in the Vietnam War. Civil rights advocates contested laws that limited housing, employment, and educational opportunities on the basis of race. They argued that these fundamental human rights were not meant to be selectively distributed based on privilege and power. Their strategies were multi-focused, in the courts, businesses, legislature, and religious institutions. Systemic change required systemic strategies but justice advocates also inspired masses of ordinary citizens, too, to resist injustice and insist on change in less systematic ways. The civil rights movement challenged the privileged classes of propertied, able-bodied white males to make room for everyone else.

The anti-Vietnam War protests also made similar challenges to authority and privilege. Draft evaders symbolized the most obvious form of resistance but they were not alone. Masses of people organized public gatherings to oppose participation in a war they considered immoral because it was motivated by political and economic gain. Though it came too late to stop a massive loss of life, public anti-war sentiment played a significant role in our final withdrawal from Vietnam.

The leaders of the civil rights and peace movements drew support from across economic, religious, and racial boundaries. People joined together to march for racial justice and to force an end to par-

---

[26] David Farber, "Introduction" in *The Sixties: From Memory to History*, ed. David Farber (Chapel Hill and London: The University of North Carolina Press, 1994) 2.

ticipation in the Vietnam War. Nothing would justify the pain incurred by victims of the war, but the force of organized masses of people, religious organizations among them, to say no to authorities with presumed unmitigated power, had made an impact. The power of ordinary people to resist what was wrong began to crack a strong, patriarchal system. There are no delusions, here. The patriarchal structure is massive, pervasive, and most of all, resistant. But, what happened, too, is irrevocable. Changes did occur when people insisted, strategized, and did not give up. David Farber points to the outcome of these efforts:

> As a result of what America did in the sixties, the United States changed dramatically. Equal opportunity became far more possible, foreign policy again was openly debated, freedom of expression exploded, America became a far more inclusive society, though an increasingly partisan cause.[27]

Though issues of gender equity were not part of public outcry at the heart of civil rights and peace movements, the cross-currents from these efforts to attain justice certainly influenced the direction, content, and momentum of the women's movement, too. Author Alice Echols argues that "many of the broad themes of the women's liberation movement—especially its concern with revitalizing the democratic process and reformulating 'politics' to include the personal—were refined and recast versions of ideas and approaches already present in the New Left and the Black freedom movement."[28] This "second phase" of the U.S. movement for women's rights, as one of the strands of civil rights, placed women's experiences in the center of the public arena: not for the first time, to be sure, but perhaps in such a way that they would not so easily be "phased out" again.

To touch ever so briefly on such a momentous time in the history of the United States, of course, does not do justice to its importance. But, the point here is simply to show the influence of the social protest movements in the 1960s on the development of feminist liturgy. Feminist liturgies, as we know them today, began at the end of the sixties in the midst of a new momentum to resist injustice and

[27] Farber, 5.
[28] Alice Echols, "Women's Liberation and Sixties Radicalism" in Farber, 151. See also Sara Evans, *Personal Politics: The Roots of Women's Liberation in the Civil Rights Movement and the New Left* (New York: Vintage Books, 1979).

to right the social balance. New, critical approaches to worship emerged when people recognized that injustice to many people, including all women, persisted in churches and synagogues.

C. "The Woman Problem"

Though different in kind and magnitude from the social protests of the 1960s, another strand of experience also played a role in the development of feminist liturgies and deserves mention here as a part of its history. This is the controversy among well-educated, middle-class women about the traditional expectation of women to be full-time homemakers. Even though only a minority of women (white middle-class and educated) were actually implicated, the topic was widely debated, especially in the media. Margaret Mead alluded to it as early as 1946: "Choose any set of criteria you like and the answer is the same: women—and men—are confused, uncertain and discontented with the present definition of women's place in America."[29]

Seventeen years later Betty Friedan became a spokesperson for white middle-class women through her *The Feminine Mystique*. Friedan pointed out that the most predominant image of women in the years after the war, one that shaped the expectations of women as well as men, was a woman who cleaned and cooked and took care of others. In fact, so identified was the image of women with cleaning that it was presumed, at least in the advertising industry, that many women found their greatest satisfaction in the wonder of household cleaners and gadgets. Something was wrong, very wrong. Through a survey of some of her Vassar classmates in 1957, Friedan discovered that this "feminine mystique" was creating a "woman problem."

> I've tried everything women are supposed to do—hobbies, gardening, pickling, canning, and being very social with my neighbors. . . . I can do it all, and I like it, but it doesn't leave you anything to think about—any feeling of who you are . . . I love the kids and Bob and my home . . . But I'm desperate. I begin to feel that I have no personality. I'm a server of food and putter-on of pants and a bedmaker, somebody who can be called on when you want something. But who am I?[30]

[29] Margaret Mead as cited in Chafe, 201.
[30] Betty Friedan, *The Feminine Mystique* (New York: Dell Publishing, 1963) 16–17.

These words resonated with millions of women, primarily those from white suburbia. Women gathered in community halls and homes to talk and share about their own experiences, using *The Feminine Mystique* as a focus. Friedan provided words for growing frustrations and grievances. Perhaps for the first time, many women saw how significantly advertisers manipulated women's image and determined their "place." Women were depicted as helpers, but even more as helpers without thoughts, critical capacities, or personal goals. Feminist liturgy intends to replace this false image with a truer one, where women act with intelligence and strength and participate in many varied ways in this world. Motivated by the belief that this understanding of women's role is consonant with God's revelation among us advocates of feminist liturgies intend to provide rituals that model and promote an authentic vision of women's dignity.

In the years following the publication of Friedan's book, it became clear that her analysis, influential as it was, was incomplete because it did not take account of differences of race, ethnicity, and class. As one working-class woman observed,

> I confess I don't feel much of a sense of sisterhood when I see pictures of Gloria Steinem . . . [a spokesperson for the movement]. . . . I feel somehow that these people don't know how it is to be getting older with very little money and education . . . it's not true that we're all in the same boat.[31]

More important to such working-class women was the need to change the prejudiced structures of a class-protected society. They wanted the opportunities for their children that white middle-class women already had. They did not envy men's professional opportunities[32] because working-class men were not respected for what they did and were often treated as less than human. As one woman said: "If your husband is a factory worker or a tugboat operator, you don't want his job. We know when they come home from work every day they feel they've been treated like the machines they operate."[33] Racial/ethnic women and working-class women were primarily concerned with economic survival and the pursuit of human dignity and justice. They had less patience, energy, and time for what many of them perceived as privileged people's issues.

[31] As cited in Hymowitz and Weissman, 362.
[32] Hymowitz and Weissman, 335.
[33] Nancy Seifer as cited in Hymowitz and Weissman, 335.

Though the 1960s were a time when people crossed barriers of race and class in pursuit of basic human rights, racial/ethnic prejudice, and varied economic experiences would continue to separate groups of women and the story of feminist liturgies reflects these divisions. There is not one story about women nor one story that includes every person. So there is not one way to ritualize. Hearing one another across critical differences, standing in solidarity beyond our own particularities and speaking honestly about varied paths of faith are some of the most complicated challenges facing those who develop feminist liturgies. Critiques of exclusion often erupt, leading to dissension and anger. Racial/ethnic women have pressed and prodded white women not to repeat the "sins of our forbears" who presumed universality at the expense of truth. Their critique has changed feminist liturgy dramatically. Knowing our varied histories provides a step, but the process toward truth-telling requires ongoing correction. The process is always changing because of what is learned along the way or as Ada Maria Isasi-Diaz writes, *en la lucha*, in the struggle for survival and liberation.[34]

D. Sexual Violence

Though identification with "the woman problem" varied among women, the conversation it sparked uncovered one aspect of women's experiences that was common to all females regardless of class, race, or education. This was the problem of violence, a reality that had been disregarded, denied and hidden. For too many women sexual violence or the fear of it is a part of daily life. When women began to talk more personally about their experiences, the prevalence of violence became more and more apparent. Examples include rape, wife-beating, sexual harassment, incest, genital mutilation, prostitution, sexual assault, and dowry death. Hardly any place is safe, not religious institutions nor public spaces nor home. In fact, most incidents happen in the privacy of homes. Violence against women and children is endemic, serious, and destructive. Susan Hagood Lee tells this story:

[34] Ada Maria Isasi-Diaz, a member of the New York Women's Liturgy Group, writes prolifically and compellingly of Hispanic women's experiences. See *En la Lucha In the Struggle: Elaborating a Mujerista Theology* (Minneapolis: Fortress Press, 1993) and *Mujerista Theology* (Maryknoll, N.Y.: Orbis Books, 1996).

From my earliest years, I was a faithful churchgoer, enjoying the religious ambiance awed by the loving and all-powerful God that I believed watched over me. Then I married a man who, once the wedding ring was safely on my finger, began to abuse me. The crisis was both personal and religious. Where was God, when one month after our wedding, my husband [a bright doctoral student in psychology] first blackened my eyes, . . . when he punched me in the stomach when I was pregnant, . . . when he broke my nose because I wanted to see my family? And what did God expect of me, a wife, who had vowed at the altar to love and cherish my husband through good times and bad?[35]

Accounts such as this one testify to what happens when men believe they have the right to use and abuse women. As in this story, God is drawn often into the picture as well. A relationship with a God, traditionally expected to be an all-powerful protector, is hard to fathom and, in fact, is confusing and upsetting, when one is being battered. Feminist liturgies intend to provide experiences that challenge crypto generalizations, "it goes with being female." They urge truth-telling, even when the truth is painful to admit. They give space for grief, wailing, arguing, confusion, and healing. The need for feminist liturgies is writ large when misuse of power reaches the level of abuse. The "right" to abuse is frightening; it is a systemic problem. Sexual violence seeps into the cracks of human relationships from many different angles: institutional practices, societal expectations, family systems, and liturgical traditions. It knows no boundaries.

E. Churches and Synagogues

Oppressive attitudes, policies, and God-talk have permeated religious organizational structures as well as secular ones.[36] Traditions

---

[35] Elizabeth Schüssler-Fiorenza and Mary Shawn Copeland, eds., *Violence Against Women* (Maryknoll, N.Y.: Orbis Books, 1994) xix.

[36] Beverly Harrison makes this connection: "The social justice radicalism of the 1960s was led by black people, whose Christianity was forged out of the distinctive experience of slavery and oppression, by Jews, by social justice-oriented Catholics, by left-wing Protestant 'sectarians,' and by secular radicals. Together, these groups began to challenge the spiritual hegemony of the U.S. Protestant mainstream. Stirrings from the 'third world' indicated further dissent from the dominant Euro-American Christian ethos. . . . The civil rights movement and the anti-Vietnam War movement signaled a renewal of praxis of world spirituality. It was within this ferment that a

that reflect gender discrimination, female inferiority and invisibility have been wrapped tightly in redemptive language. Any change threatens to upset the understanding of God's saving work on our behalf.[37]

Overcoming centuries of discrimination requires time, study, conversation, strategizing, and commitment. But even more is required. Beverly Harrison asserts that changing such deeply-rooted convictions demands the "power of anger in the work of love."[38] "A chief evidence of the grace of God," says Harrison, "is this power to struggle and experience indignation. We should not make light of our power to rage against the dying of the light. It is the root of the power of love."[39] To challenge traditional religious interpretations at the heart of our beliefs is difficult and at times, disturbing. It requires the fuel of indignation to cry out for justice and to keep on struggling in the face of powerful resistance. The process often involves saying "no" to something before we know the "yes" to what is new or emerging.

The most visible and well-published struggles for justice within church and synagogue relate to language, interpretations of sacred texts, and leadership. In this section, I will sketch some of the transitional and critical moments in U.S. religious history with regard to leadership and, in particular, the ordination of women. The following chapter discusses questions about other components of liturgical expressions.

In most churches and synagogues significant ritual actions are led by ordained members. In some, ordination is required to validate these sacramental expressions. Ordained leaders make decisions about what will be said and heard and done by the members of their

---

woman's movement emerged, affecting church women, who then demanded fuller direct participation in the church's ministry." Beverly Harrison, *Making the Connections: Essays in Feminist Social Ethics* (Boston: Beacon Press, 1985) 223.

[37] Delores Williams boldly asserts the connections between theologies of atonement, which emphasize that Jesus died on the cross to save humankind, and women's passive acceptance of their own suffering. To look carefully at an understanding of traditional teachings about redemption in churches and to acknowledge its effect on women's experiences is required so that violence never is understood as the will of God. See Delores S. Williams, *Sisters in the Wilderness* (Maryknoll: Orbis, 1993).

[38] Harrison, 3.

[39] Harrison, 20–21.

congregations. Ordained clergy are most often the visible, public representatives of the religious community at large. Their representative power and decision-making are critical in shaping symbols of religious commitment within the church or synagogue. They have talent and trained perspectives to offer. Including women in ordained leadership positions is critical to right the imbalance in any denomination where male clergy dominate. Women must be intrepid in this quest. Power is not handed over easily.

As early as the American revolution women led religious communities. Laywomen pressed for authority in their local congregations as well as in regional and national meetings. Though they knew well the prohibition against women speaking in mixed groups, nevertheless, they asked to speak, to vote, and to serve on governing boards of congregations.[40]

In these early stages most discussions about women's participation in religious congregations focused on questions about women's ordained and/or preaching ministry in Protestant churches. Women in newly-established independent churches and in predominantly black churches played significant roles in taking positions of leadership. Records show that a former slave woman named Elizabeth preached as early as 1796. She depended on no human authority to give approbation. When asked if she was ordained, she responded, "Not by the commission of men's hands; if the Lord has ordained me, I need nothing better."[41] As in the early Church, women of a variety of religious convictions, including Quakers and Shakers, kept congregations going with financial contributions and hospitality. At times they served as itinerant evangelists. "Women did what needed to be done or what seemed led by the Spirit and nobody objected."[42]

By the nineteenth century Julia A. Foote, the first black woman in the A.M.E. Zion Church (1809), and Antoinette Brown, the first white woman in a Congregational church (1853), had been formally ordained. A few others followed in churches that did not require a larger denominational body to approve ordination, e.g., Northern Baptists, Unitarians, and Disciples of Christ. But, not until the mid-twentieth century did questions of ordained ministry begin

---

[40] Barbara Brown Zikmund in Rosemary Radford Ruether and Rosemary Skinner Keller, *In Our Own Voices; Four Centuries of American's Women's Religious Writing* (San Francisco: HarperSanFrancisco, 1995) 293.

[41] Zikmund, in Ruether and Keller, 304.

[42] Zikmund, in Ruether and Keller, 294.

to infiltrate the governing structures of other Protestant churches and finally lead to the inclusion of female ministers and priests among the ordained.

In seeking ordination Protestant women led the way. Reform Jewish women followed. By the mid-nineteenth century Reform Jews, led by Isaac Meyer Wise, had incorporated significant changes in women's participation in the synagogue. They counted women as full members of the congregation, changed the practice of separate seating in the back of the sanctuary and provided access to religious education. Rabbi Wise even encouraged changing the marriage vows so that women did not "obey" their husbands, but rather entered into a reciprocal covenant with them. Wise did not stop here but also pressed for women's right to vote and to be ordained. Neither happened in his lifetime. Reform Jews would wait until 1972 to ordain Sally Priesand their first female rabbi. Reconstructionist Jews followed suit in ordaining women two years later and Conservative Jews in 1985.[43]

The process has been much less satisfying for Roman Catholics. When Vatican Council II enjoined *all* Catholics to be more actively involved in the Church and in the liturgy, many Catholics took this invitation seriously. Roman Catholic women, women religious as well as laywomen, began a long and irreversible journey to become visible agents in many arenas of the Church's life. Though in some churches women have assumed leadership, all ordinary sacramental leadership remains reserved to men. Decades later there is still only debate about ordination of women and, more recently, an official statement that even prohibits discussion of the question.

Feminist liturgies developed in the midst of these struggles to admit female clergy. The justice expressed in a more inclusive clergy is related to the justice of a more inclusive liturgy. When a woman leads worship, her presence makes visible a God who is not known more adequately through men. When a woman prays in the name of the community, she illustrates quite tangibly that no particular sound can be called "God's sound." When women offer their own perspectives on the living realities of faith, they reinforce the differences every person adds to interpretations of texts, symbols, and sacramental actions. The ordination of women has made an enormous difference in the lives of religious congregations. But issues of

[43] See Ann Braude, "Women and Religious Practice in American Judaism" in Ruether and Keller, 110–52.

ordination are only one part of the struggle to express our relationships with God, one another, and other creatures more fully and more truthfully.

When women began to understand that liturgy was being done "for us" rather than "with us," when women continued to hear ourselves mentioned in denigrating stereotypes—among them, a defective human being, the source of temptation, or a whore—when women realized that they rarely, if ever, heard anything of what other women thought or experienced, when women recognized that God was continually imaged in male words even after repeated discussions of the destructive implications of this practice, we knew something had to change. We knew, too, that if it was going to happen, we had to be the ones to do it and we would have to begin outside official structures.

The movement to imagine these liturgical changes began in the late 1960s, when women, and some men, too, gathered to imagine and celebrate liturgies that utilized a broader spectrum of human experience in order to express the actions of God among us. We came together from specific denominations, across different faiths and, in some cases, from minimal religious background. Some groups originated in academic settings, others in churches and synagogues. We met in homes, basements, outdoors, and in various community places. We convened to create space, time, and opportunities to explore questions of faith, such as "What does the Bible tell me about my freedom as a daughter of God? How do I see my womanhood as a reflection of God? Who are the women I want to imitate? How do I as a woman experience sin? What does it mean to be a woman?"[44] We knew that something vital was missing in the traditions we had inherited. We came together to figure out what that was by exploring something different, sharing responses to ongoing questions, and supporting one another in an uncharted journey.

In the intervening thirty years what we knew intuitively at first has been clarified, interpreted, developed, and corrected. Participants in this process have talked regularly and honestly with each other about what works and what does not. Academics have offered historical, biblical, theological, and sociological data to undergird what we only guessed was true. People from the secular women's movement and others alienated from any official religious structures have

---

[44] *Sistercelebrations: Nine Worship Experiences*, ed. Arlene Swidler (Philadelphia: Fortress Press, 1974) v.

offered strategies to stretch our traditional ways of forming communities. What has emerged is a new liturgical vision. This belief and practice is what we know as feminist liturgy.

2 Feminist Liturgy: Its Tasks and Principles

The tasks and principles of feminist liturgy developed in this matrix of historical and social change. They are rooted in a dialogue between history and liturgy, that is, between the realities of history and the expectations and potential of liturgy. They express the webbing of awareness and hope.

Feminist liturgy seeks to engage imagination, resist discrimination, summon wonder, receive blessing and strengthen hope. It intends to enact redeemed, free and empowered relationships. Feminist liturgy builds on basic assumptions:

> we come together to name what is "true" for us;
> we invite one another to listen, speak, and act;
> we know God as constant surprise, more than what we've
>   been taught, more than we can imagine;
> we use a variety of forms and resources, traditional and
>   emerging;
> we anticipate new awarenesses and change;
> we resist whatever demeans or hurts;
> we account to each other for what we do;
> we struggle with differences;
> we play as we pray;
> we expect to embody justice for ourselves, our world, and God.

Our goal, as liturgical scholar Mary Collins states, is to "ritualize relationships that emancipate and empower women,"[1] and subsequently

---

[1] Mary Collins, "Principles of Feminist Liturgy" in *Women at Worship: Interpretations of North American Diversity,* ed. Marjorie Procter-Smith and Janet Roland Walton (Louisville: Westminster/John Knox Press, 1993) 9.

all those marginalized by class, race, differing abilities, sexual orientations, and age.

Because feminist liturgy began in the wake of the second phase of the women's movement, with an explicit scrutinizing of ways in which women fared in all aspects of society, we use the word "feminist" to describe it. Women's experiences are focal. They provide a critical lens to understand all kinds of exclusion and harm. Though a patriarchal perspective limited the participation of most people, it actually excluded *all* women. Sharon Neufer Emswiler, one of the early pioneers in feminist liturgy, put it this way:

> When the worship hour is concluded I leave the church wondering, "Why am I going away feeling less human than when I came?" That which should have created a sense of wholeness in me made me feel dehumanized, less than a full person. What was meant to be a time of worship of the true God was, for me, a worship of the masculine—the masculine experience among humans and the masculine dimension of God.[2]

During the almost thirty years of the development of feminist liturgies women have learned that the changes we have incorporated into our ritualizing has radically altered what we expect from liturgical experiences. In the beginning we knew only that what we inherited was not true, that is, to know the revelation of God only through male experiences was not credible any longer. But we had no sense of what would emerge when we tried to broaden the spectrum of expression, that is, to do liturgy differently. Now we understand that when we listen to one another we can shape liturgical experiences that honor rather than demean, that correct what hurts and that make consistent efforts to embody justice.

Our liturgies are not perfect; our learning continually evolves. A description of what we say about feminist liturgies will inevitably be incomplete because what we enact is shaped by changing lives. We are always practicing, a practicing Ronald Grimes defines as "the action of attending . . . to what presents itself."[3]

In this section I discuss what we have realized together. What we have come to understand includes unfolding perspectives about

[2] Sharon Neufer Emswiler and Thomas Neufer Emswiler, *Women and Worship: A Guide to Non-Sexist Hymns, Prayers and Liturgies* (New York: Harper & Row, 1974) 3.

[3] Ronald L. Grimes, *Marrying and Burying: Rites of Passage in a Man's Life* (Boulder, Co.: Westview Press, 1995) 220.

honoring one another and God, correcting what has limited such honoring, and doing liturgy differently. My intention is to describe feminist liturgical tasks and principles so they, in turn, can contribute to discussions about *all* our liturgies. What we have learned is not for ourselves only but for any communities who want to improve their attempts to ritualize relationships, divine and human and other-kind.

A. Honoring One Another and God

Fundamental to the understanding of feminist liturgy is a simple fact: since people are different, the naming and cherishing of our differences is essential in our liturgical experiences. For many centuries following dominant cultural norms, the language of liturgies did not take distinctions into account. Feminist liturgies seek to change this habit. Honoring various experiences recognizes more fully what each person knows about being human and about relating to God. When anyone is invisible, aspects of God, too, are also rendered invisible.

Our liturgies rely on various languages: words, space, gestures, and sounds. What we say and read, whom and what we look at, and the ways in which we use our bodies; all of these factors communicate what we believe and influence how we act. Verbal language, especially the predominance of male imagery, offered one of the first clues to many of us that something was wrong with our institutional liturgies. Many resources have become available that offer informed, detailed discussions about the languages of liturgies, their problems and their possibilities.[4] Because changing long-established traditions of language requires care, respect, and in the end, movement into uncharted paths, study, and conversation are essential to our attempts to right this wrong. Listed below are some examples of what we discovered when we began to shape feminist liturgies. These samples will inevitably suggest others.

[4] Many references are available. Among them: Marjorie Procter-Smith, *In Her Own Rite: Constructing Feminist Liturgical Tradition* (Nashville: Abingdon Press, 1990); Gail Ramshaw, *Liturgical Language: Keeping It Metaphoric, Making It Inclusive* (Collegeville: The Liturgical Press, 1996); Casey Miller and Kate Swift, *Words and Women: New Language in New Times,* rev. ed. (San Francisco: HarperCollins, 1991); Heather Murray Elkins, *Worshipping Women: Reforming God's People For Praise* (Nashville: Abingdon Press, 1994).

1. Words

When we name ourselves precisely as women, girls, sisters, and daughters, several experiences happen at the same time. We think about what these particular relationships mean to us. We are not sons, brothers, men, or boys, though for many years, by reason of male power and preference, we've heard ourselves described as such. We are daughters, sisters, girls, females with quite distinctive experiences socially, physically, and relationally. These differences matter. As we talk about these experiences, we begin not only to claim our distinctions as females but also to respect and enjoy them. With respect comes power, both personal and collective. We have the strength to act from what we know: to seek what energizes us and to say no to anything that diminishes or hurts us. This kind of authority is what we expect to provide one another in feminist liturgies.

No longer can we accept words about our identity as females that are subsumed in male terms such as mankind, man, sons, or brothers. Males and females share humanness. Together we constitute the human species. Male terms for males and females are confusing and demeaning. Lexicographer Alma Graham puts it this way:

> If a woman is swept into the water, the cry is "man overboard." If she is killed by a hit-and-run driver, the charge is "manslaughter." If she is injured on the job, the coverage is "workmen's compensation." But if she arrives at a threshold marked "Men Only," she knows the admonition is not intended to bar animals or plants or inanimate objects. It is meant for her.[5]

Feminist liturgies expect accuracy. They reject words that support deception and distortion and violence. "Man" is no less partial than "woman," just as clearly as "white" is no less partial than "black" or "brown," "red" or "yellow." Naming females precisely is critical to reversing dishonesty. It is just one step toward honoring females, no doubt, but it also protects all of us from recurring harm. No one can presume power over women; nor are females required to give it. Precision in naming speeds a process of truth telling and faithful relationships. It is an act of justice.

Another example of inaccuracy that leads to discrimination is color-coded language. The common use of the color "black" to de-

---

[5] Alma Graham as cited in Casey Miller and Kate Swift, *Words and Women: New Language in New Times* (Garden City: Anchor Books, 1977) 25.

scribe or refer to what is bad or evil supports fear and suspiciousness of black people. In a racist society, color-coded language promotes a bias that black people are evil, more prone to violence and sin than whites. We honor one another when we stop using any words that vilify one another.

In a similar way, language that connects able-bodied people to goodness and disabled people to sin (I am blind, but now I see) dishonors. As Valerie Stiteler points out, "As long as images of body disability [blindness, deafness, lameness] are used negatively . . . few of the disabled . . . can participate fully in worship or receive the salvation offered to all humans."[6]

Words that categorize people dehumanize them as well. One such example is references to people by adjectives without nouns. I refer to expressions like "the poor," "the homeless," "the blind." We are speaking about *people in our midst* for whom we are all accountable. They are poor people, homeless people, people who are blind. They are women, men, and children—not a lump of unknown, general, convenient groupings of marginalized beings. No one is less human for being sense-impaired or out of luck.

Age is also a stereotypical cause of discrimination in our culture. The young and the old are the primary victims. Teenagers are seen as rude and cynical and old or retired people are perceived to be out of step. Institutional liturgies rarely use emerging or ancient metaphors that express the wisdom of varying ages, e.g., "crone" to evoke the wisdom of aging women. Feminist liturgies seek to counter cultural presuppositions about age.

Finally, feminist liturgies challenge words and practices that dishonor God. There is always a danger of making God what we want rather than accepting what God is. We know God as ever more than we can conceive. Feminist liturgies attempt to guard against limiting God to what we want, whether it be part of a long-accepted tradition or what we desire to be "right." We hope to avoid measuring ourselves against an image of our own making. "All images are necessarily partial," writes Marcia Falk, "the authentic expression of a monotheism is not a singularity of image but an embracing unity of a multiplicity of images, as many as are needed to express and reflect

---

[6] Valerie C. Jones Stiteler, "Singing Without a Voice: Using Disability Images in the Language of Public Worship" in *The Anna Howard Shaw Center Newsletter* 8:1 (Fall 1991).

the diversity of our individual lives."[7] Not even names we have used for thousands of years can possibly convey the total reality of God. To believe otherwise is idolatrous. A continual process of naming God seems more consistent with an ever-revealing God than a tendency to employ only a few traditional names for the divine. Feminist liturgies aspire to act on this premise.

Naming what we know or are coming to know about God is a critical part of the process of feminist liturgy. As Marjorie Procter-Smith points out, naming God is "urgent and primary because liturgy is not reflection but address; an encounter is presumed."[8] Feminist liturgy is more than talk; it is enacting relationships that promote justice among us and beyond us. When we meet we call out to each other and to God; we expect to show God to each other. Liturgy is a "showing of a doing,"[9] an action in which we try to "be" what we do. As such it requires constant examination and experimentation.

2. Space: Objects and Arrangements

Not only our words but also what we see matters in the performance of feminist liturgies. Because women regularly gather in each other's homes, in places that women often have some part in designing, we noticed immediately that we enjoyed this new (but, in reality, ancient) environment for our liturgies. In a place decorated with things we cherish, objects that encourage our memories, pictures of families and friends who are our forebears, symbols that evoke all kinds of stories, we knew quickly how important the physical space was in our gatherings.

This recognition leads to wondrous care about the environment of liturgy. As in our homes, in our feminist liturgies we want our space to be evocative, honest, connected to our everyday lives, all its heartaches, terrors and accomplishments; as well as what we yearn to know and be. In planning our liturgies we intentionally gather whatever we need to meet this goal, whether it be pictures, objects, or traditional liturgical symbols such as water, candles, oil, or food.

[7] Marcia Falk, "Notes on Composing New Blessings: Toward a Feminist Jewish Reconstruction of Prayer" in *The Journal of Feminist Studies in Religion,* 3:1 (Spring 1987) 41

[8] Procter-Smith (1990) 88.

[9] Tom F. Driver develops this concept amply and compellingly in his book, *Liberating Rites: Understanding the Transformative Power of Ritual* (Boulder, Co.: Westview Press, 1998).

Some things are used once; others reappear regularly. Each time we expect the symbols to disclose layer upon layer of meanings, e.g., a wreath of unadorned boughs may remind us primarily about the dying of life at one liturgy, and, at another time, the same wreath, decorated differently with bright colors or unfolding buds, may accent the living of life. We explore multiple aspects of the objects we use with the intention of knowing, and sometimes being surprised by their fresh connections.

Because we know that part of any dynamic relationship is to uncover more and more about the "other" we experiment with images of God, too. We learn from trying; making new pictures or shapes, using found objects in original arrangements, uncovering nuances in traditional visualizations and most of all, from listening to each other, hearing about images that make connections with what is ultimately holy. Though we certainly know we cannot contain the essence of God with any real accuracy, we do know we can deepen our own relationships through a never-ending process of imagining.

Objects are one aspect of the environment, while another is the arrangement of ourselves in the space. Most often we try to arrange the furniture so that we can be near each other. All of us are primary visible agents of each other's freedom and development. We are all images of God. We do not want to look away from each other nor establish great distances from each other. Though there are leaders who volunteer to prepare and guide each liturgy, the arrangement of the space does not privilege any person over another as if any person has an edge on holiness, God, or special knowing. The arrangement of space is the first invitation in liturgies. Too often it separates us rather than unites us. We recognize its power to transform our work together.

3. Gestures[10]

Horizontal gestures prevail in feminist liturgies; they suggest equality and interdependence; they affirm God known among us. Generally we do not look up to find God. We connect with each other to give and receive blessings.

We pray with our eyes open and without bowing our heads. Not that we do not acknowledge God's authority, but we know God does

---

[10] Much of what is included here is from an important article by Marjorie Procter-Smith, "Reorganizing Victimization: The Intersection between Liturgy and Domestic Violence" in *The Perkins Journal* (October 1987) 17–27.

not require bowing our heads and closing our eyes. Bowing our heads for a blessing, as Marjorie Procter-Smith points out, is "a non-reciprocal action"[11] related to experiences that remind us of male domination. It signals an inferior social status that has not promoted women's well-being. Closing one's eyes is dangerous in an unjust society. Though we presume we are safe in our gatherings, we do not repeat actions that have historically limited, demeaned or hurt us.

Kneeling poses problems, too. We recognize its value to remind us of reverence for God and one another, but when women kneel to receive Communion or a blessing from men, rather than promoting an experience of reverence, it can be a reminder of sexual violation or subservience. Since women are frequently victims of violence at the hands of men, we practice standing and sitting rather than kneeling. We want to remind ourselves every time we can that sexual violence is rooted in misplaced power, that is, when anyone presumes power over another. Feminist liturgies intend to provide occasions to practice gestures of resistance and expressions of shared power.

4. Sounds

No particular sounds characterize feminist liturgies, but some guidelines frame our choices. We search for music that has been forgotten, composers or performers made invisible throughout history because of their marginalization. We consciously include music of many styles, such as drumming, chanting, wailing, rapping, as well as a variety of instruments, especially percussion. We reject songs with texts or tunes that limit or demean anyone; we rewrite words to familiar, well-known or well-loved melodies; and sometimes, we commission new songs to meet particular needs.

5. Movement

Whereas in many institutional liturgies we limit our movements to processions or changing our postures, in feminist liturgies we make conscious efforts to engage the resources of our bodies more fully. Though we may be self-conscious and awkward, we dance, we move together, we touch each other in actions of solidarity, play, and blessing. We value the revelations of our bodies along a wide spectrum of abilities and disabilities.

[11] Procter-Smith (1987) 25.

The first phase of the tasks and principles of feminist liturgies, honoring God, ourselves, one another and other-kind, involved naming what was inaccurate, distinguishing what was true, believing what we learned, and resisting naysayers. The next phase required correction. Honoring and correcting are inextricably intertwined.

B. Correcting the Limits Imposed by Patriarchy

1. Self-image

One of the most serious and pervasive by-products of a patriarchal, androcentric (male-focused) culture is self-doubt, and even self-hatred, among females. People who are excluded and marginalized deduce that they have little to contribute to others. At times, they hate themselves. Institutions and individuals reinforce these misconceptions when they do not stop the traditions that isolate power of all sorts to a few people. Correcting this imbalance is a life-long endeavor. It requires personal attentiveness and collective power. Delores Williams describes her own journey toward "self-invention":

> I suddenly realized that if I, a black woman, was going to be free and liberated, I had to create myself *into* that [self-invention] freedom. The process has been continuous. It is full of mistakes, of being knocked down and getting up, of bending but being determined not to break, of delving into the innermost reaches of my spirit. It is full of discovery; of discovering a strong and resilient faith in God, of finding support from that deity and from communities of women—black and white—and from my family.[12]

Feminist liturgies attend persistently to this activity of "self-invention," which is a constant unwrapping of what is true and a correction of what is not. It is arduous work in a society ill-equipped and unwilling to perceive the need to alter its expressions of power and authority. This task of "self-invention" is demanding among women in particular. Women are often complicit in misusing power, in restricting other women's struggle to self-invention. This situation occurs when we are unwilling to see and hear how our different racial, class histories, experiences of bodily conditions and sexual orientations shape struggles for self-invention. Women of color,

---

[12] Delores Williams, "Women as Makers of Literature" in *Women's Spirit Bonding*, ed. Janet Kalven and Mary I. Buckley (New York: Pilgrim Press, 1988) 141–42.

women with various disabilities, women from working classes regularly offer corrections to white middle-class women when feminist liturgies presume a norm that applies to all women. This dialogue among women is difficult and at times divisive but it is critical to the task of truth-telling and the pursuit of justice.

What makes change possible is a community of people doing this work together: speaking honestly, offering support, pointing out possibilities, evoking the strengths of one another, and enduring in spite of resistance. When one or another is down and discouraged, someone else helps. When one or another succeeds, the community rejoices. A collective struggle carries amazing and necessary persistence. Feminist liturgies, like all ritualizing, provide repeated occasions to identify and let go of false self-images. Repetition, a context for regularly challenging destructive habits, is a crucial step toward new awareness and helps to lift off the layers of self-doubt.

Times of "not-knowing" are part of this process of self-invention. They are acceptable and expected in feminist liturgies. Although the self-image women inherited was demeaning, it was the only one we knew. We were socialized to think it was true. To correct it requires a tumbling about, with little direction, free-fall where everything, it seems, all habits of thinking, speaking, listening, behaving, are questioned. The times marked by rhythms: cutting away, loneliness, and experimenting, over and over.

Silence and lament are partners in the struggles toward truth. We await one another in feminist liturgies. We have learned that silent time is fertile space, necessary for attentiveness, dreaming and imagining. We lament our losses of all kinds: familiar forms of liturgy, songs we sing by heart, work we do in our churches and synagogues, and relationships that offer a particular kind of security. While we miss the collective power of large numbers of people, the beauty of hearty sounds, the inspiration of well-done ceremonies, and the stimulation of lofty architecture, we recognize that too often these good things often come packaged with expressions of dominance, diminishment and exclusion. But, our lament does not end here. It also includes stopping our excessive giving.

Delores Williams points out that lamentation is needed "not only because of things I could not do or was denied . . . As a Black woman, I 'sang' lamentations for the times I'd given too much because I did not know better":[13]

---

[13] Delores Williams in Kalven and Buckley, 141–42.

                    things I've shut my life to
                           coming up fast
             like quick rain and summer sun
                    gettin' use to hindsight
                      instead of foresight
                    youth beauty wanting
                            and dreaming
               fading into aunti mamma
                         and hard times
                  getting use to my man
            promising the best he can
                               half way
         loving and bleeding and aching
                            like a tooth
                  that never gets fixed
                              just right
            I shut my life to things
             like candy and flowers
                      and touching.
                At a just right time.[14]

Our silence and our laments are deeply engaged and wide-reaching. They are another source of power.

Feminist liturgies offer a regular opportunity for self-invention through a particular kind of "knowing." We learn, not so much by way of discussion, although that may be a by-product of what we do, but rather by *doing* our ritualizing differently. We enact another way of relating to ourselves, others, and God. Our understanding changes our performance.

For women particularly, this performance of a corrected self-image requires a recovery of every aspect of our embodied selves. We are not bodies disassociated from our minds. We are not primarily pencil-thin, media-normed shaped objects. Feminist liturgies intend to resist exploitation of female bodies, whether by our own self-deceptions or others' judgmental appraisals. We work to cherish our different shapes, large and small, in various conditions and colors. We intend to honor women who have had to undergo body-changing surgery in order to save their lives. We aim to model beauty differently, making a habit of respecting and loving our bodies and

[14] Delores Williams, unpublished manuscript, to be published in *Songs I Meant to Sing.*

41

minds. As we discover and accept truer images of ourselves, we inevitably seek truer images of God.

2. God's Image

The process of naming God requires similar correction: letting go, lamenting, trying something new, adjusting, and trying again. We mourn familiar terms or names that have been comforting to us, e.g., for some of us, the word "Father" for God. But, we have discovered that comfort can be deceiving as well. It keeps us from owning relationships with God that were consistent with our developing understanding of ourselves and our relationships. Humans are expected to be accountable agents of creation, initiated by God, yes, but continued by us. We call upon God differently when we are children or young adults. We call upon God differently as responsible participants in the shaping of our world. Our names for God reflect such changing relationships.

As liturgical scholar Mary Collins says, "an uncritical cherishing of androcentric images of God in public prayer at the end of the twentieth century is self-indulgent, whether men or women do the cherishing."[15] But the work of correction is not without consequences. Collins wisely warns, "if we are willing to take up a self-critical stance . . . , we are in danger of being left speechless in our liturgical assemblies-stumbling over our words as Jeremiah and many other mystics have done: Ah . . . I do not know how to speak" (Jer 1:6).[16] Maybe this fear is the one we dread most, the not knowing, the waiting in silence.

The construction of feminist liturgies includes wrestling with many questions about naming and knowing God. Some examples include: What are the boundaries of changes in the trinitarian formula?[17] When shall we call upon God in female terms, mother, sister, goddess? How do we discover emerging names, constructed from changing experiences of a living God? How do we avoid sanctioning abuse, e.g., the use of "Father" as the most often heard name

---

[15] Mary Collins, *Worship: Renewal to Practice* (Washington, D.C.: Pastoral Press, 1987) 228.

[16] Collins (1987) 228.

[17] See Ruth C. Duck, *Gender and the Name of God* (New York: The Pilgrim Press, 1991) and Gail Ramshaw, *God beyond Gender* (Minneapolis: Fortress/Augsburg, 1995).

for God may suggest to victims of sexual abuse wittingly or unwittingly that like an abusing father God cannot be trusted. What must we let go? What shall we add? When is silence the most honest way to identify one who is "more" than we can imagine? The work of naming God is pivotal to the development of feminist liturgy.

Feminist liturgy seeks to correct what for so long has been acceptable through creating awarenesses of inherent injustice and of the limits that "continuing as usual" imposes on the truth of our liturgies. The liturgies model another way. Self-images and God-images need immediate correction. Remembering and telling stories are also a part of the process of healing and change.

3. Stories

Most institutional liturgies, as dictated by the patriarchal structure in which they were created, focused on men's stories and men's contributions, myths that isolated and honored men's achievements. To our surprise we realized that we, too, had become accustomed to hearing the biblical stories of Moses, Abraham, Isaac, Jacob, Matthew, Mark, Luke, John, and Paul. Where were Miriam, Sarah, Hagar, Rebecca, Leah, Rachel, Phoebe, Dorcas, and Prisca? For thousands of years we had never noticed they were missing. Why were they left out? When women were included, why were the interpretations so distorted? How could all females be unnecessary witnesses for succeeding generations except as sources of sin and temptation? Missing names and misinterpreted stories are a critical problem for a liturgical community. As Marjorie Procter-Smith says, "Without them as part of our living memory and of our liturgical memorials, we have no measure against which to judge who we are or who we might be."[18]

An enormous outpouring of research in recent years has begun to correct this historical inaccuracy. Biblical scholars, historians, theologians, and liturgists have provided extensive resources. The following small sampling of familiar biblical references makes the point clear. Stories from many other sources are in the next section.

a. Mary of Magdala has been traditionally pictured, named, and experienced liturgically most frequently as a whore and a sinner (Luke 7:36-50). Biblical scholar Elizabeth Schüssler-Fiorenza, who

---

[18] Procter-Smith (1990) 36.

has dedicated much of her research to a feminist biblical interpretation,[19] points out that this image prevails over the image of Mary of Magdala as a faithful friend of Jesus, the first to recognize the risen Christ because biblical interpretation has been influenced by the male-dominated world view that restricted women's roles and power and visibility. Schüssler-Fiorenza and other scholars offer a reading of biblical texts that point to what communities have forgotten, have misread and have rejected.[20] At best, our understandings of biblical persons are guesses, even when undergirded by substantial research. Communities of faith are served well when we see women through multiple lenses; from the perspective of the context in which they lived, the mind set and literary skills of the writers and our own experiences. Mary of Magdala is more accurately presented as a complex human being like all the disciples of Jesus, imperfect yet courageous enough to venture forth to anoint Jesus. Hers was a simple expression of care and love.

b. The story of Eve and Adam, biblical scholar Phyllis Trible demonstrates, is primarily about "life and death," "a love story gone awry," in which life has lost to death, harmony to hostility, unity and fulfillment to fragmentation and dispersion.[21] This Genesis text relates to many more aspects of our human lives than the limited but more prevalent reading that Eve (and thus every woman) is the source of all temptation. It is a foundational myth, one that helps to uncover the many-layered meanings of the daily challenges of our lives as well as the constant and varied reappearances of the rhythms of living and dying.

c. The daughter of Jephthah (Judg 11:29-40) and an unnamed woman (Judg 19:1-30) are examples of abuse of women. The daughter of Jephthah was given as a sacrifice in return for her father's winning

---

[19] Elizabeth Schüssler-Fiorenza's *In Memory of Her* (New York: Crossroad, 1983) was a groundbreaking book in feminist biblical reconstruction. Since then there have been others that developed and extended these same themes. Among them: *But She Said* (Boston: Beacon Press, 1992) and *Jesus: Miriam's Child, Sophia's Prophet* (New York: Continuum, 1994).

[20] *The Women's Bible Commentary*, ed. Carol A. Newsom and Sharon H. Ringe (Louisville: Westminster/John Knox Press, 1992), is an accessible, dependable resource for helpful information and critical interpretations.

[21] Phyllis Trible, *God and the Rhetoric of Sexuality* (Philadelphia: Fortress Press, 1978) 72–143.

of a war. The unnamed concubine from Bethlehem was gang-raped as entertainment for the men of the town. Neither story is commonly part of the Sunday liturgies when most people would hear them. Yet they ring with familiarity to many women.[22] Reading them is critical to put an end to the silence about physical and sexual abuse.

d. Hagar is known in biblical history as the surrogate mother who replaced Sarah, Abraham's wife, in order for Abraham to sire a son (Gen 16:1-16; 21:9-21). Hagar bore Ishmael and was eventually cast off with her son at the request of Sarah. African-American women have seen parallels with their own lives. They, too, bore children for their masters. They, too, were treated brutally by white women who employed them. Hagar's determination to survive despite all odds, even the absence of God, has been life-giving to black women. But, as Delores Williams points out, "liberation in the Hagar stories is not given by God; it finds its source in human initiative."[23]

Hearing such stories read on Sundays and discovering interpretations free from patriarchal bias, invites both women and men to think deeply and afresh about our own stories of faith, about our own behavior and our own understandings of human dignity and blessing as well as inferiority, blame, sin, and suffering. These stories lead us to ask questions about our talk about God, too: How is God present among us? When does God not save us? What does such an absence mean?

Storytelling and passing on inherited myths are wondrous capacities of humans. Misuse of stories deprives the whole human community of what is true. Correction of these habits requires vigilance, humility, persistence, and openness.

C. Doing Liturgy Differently

Since we come together to invite each other to listen, to speak and to act, feminist liturgies require participation that is reciprocal, accountable, and relational. Every person contributes to the action

---

[22] See Phyllis Trible, *Texts of Terror: Literary-Feminist Readings of Biblical Narratives* (Philadelphia: Fortress Press, 1984) for an in-depth interpretation and analysis of these and other similar texts.

[23] Delores Williams, *Sisters in the Wilderness: The Challenge of Womanist God-Talk* (Maryknoll, N.Y.: Orbis Books, 1993) 7.

though in different proportions at different times, but each shares some responsibility for what happens. No one embodies God's invitation to us more than any other. Every person counts.

1. Feminist Participation Is Reciprocal

Whereas in a patriarchal ritual one or a few men traditionally mediate power to and from God and to and from the people, feminist ritualizing eliminates the impression that there is an elite group on whom divine power and presence depends. Not that feminist liturgies exclude ordained leaders, but they do presume that each person is needed, ordained or not. The whole community draws out the interaction with each other and with God. Leadership is reordered as collective authority, and power is imaged in new ways.

The primary task of leaders in feminist liturgies is to set a context in which everyone can participate, to provide opportunities for a variety of kinds of participation. The goal is a spirit of celebration in which each person knows that she or he depends on another, learns from another, and evokes the other. All kinds of expertise are needed and welcome.

2. Feminist Participation Is Accountable

Closely related to reciprocity is accountability. It is not enough to participate actively when it feels good or is convenient. At the heart of feminist liturgies is *collective* work. They require being there for each other, in good times and bad. They presume that we listen, speak, and act. But, they do not presume we will always "get it right." In order to avoid the mistake of continuing what has always been done because it is familiar and comfortable, at the center of our commitment to feminist liturgies is both experimentation and regular critique. What does not work is not repeated.

3. Feminist Participation Is Relational

Feminist liturgy seeks to summarize the discoveries reported in this section. It intends "to actualize redeemed and redeeming relationships that allow women [and all marginalized people] to claim their full power as human persons."[24] To ensure empowered rela-

---

[24] Collins, in Procter-Smith and Walton, 11.

tionships in a culture that resists change, Mary Collins suggests four moments in a process:

> *suspicion* in approaching all cultural materials, especially those considered to be a particular culture's highest achievements, *retrieval* of aspects of women's cultural experience of all kinds of significant relationships, *affirmation* of what has been retrieved both of women's achievements and stories of women's suffering exacted as the price of maintaining patriarchal relationships, and *introducing a future* that affirms the full humanity of women and the value and truth of their achievements.[25]

Ultimately, feminist liturgy is about making available for one another an embodied vision of relationships rooted in valuing each person, drawing collective strength from each other and from the presence and promises of the Holy One. This vision expands regularly because feminist liturgy is organic, that is, it continually evolves around data from our lives. As our lives change so, too, do the content and form of our liturgies. Texts are not read because they are assigned or because an authority outside our own requires it. Likewise nothing is eliminated merely because it is part of a long tradition. Something is read because it is assumed there will be a connection with the ways we live and die. Something is heard with the hope that it will evoke a fresh insight or a powerful memory. Something is done as fuel for an act of resistance for what we do beyond the ritual space. Every component of the liturgy is evaluated from this perspective. The way we live and die is inextricably connected to an understanding of an unpredictable transcendent being, one who is known intimately and expected to be revealed in our midst.

Feminist liturgies and perspectives span a wide spectrum of expressions, but they are all about inviting and receiving one another as images of God. In these interactions a new vision emerges, not a perfect one, not a whole one, but rather one that we can use for a while as an alternative to an outmoded vision that has excluded marginalized persons, especially all women.

---

[25] Collins, in Procter-Smith and Walton, 12.

3 Feminist Liturgy: The Possibilities It Offers

The development of feminist liturgies has proceeded in stages. Changes in language were the easiest and most obvious first steps. But as women began to look more and more carefully at what was happening in institutional liturgies, it became clear that language was just the tip of the iceberg. What follows are samples of feminist liturgies that exemplify some aspects of what has evolved. They are intended to provide concrete examples of what we mean when we identify a liturgy as feminist.

Integral to the process of feminist liturgy is a premise that the content and forms of the liturgy are intimately connected to the lives of the people who gather to ritualize. As a result, what is published here, or in fact anywhere, is not meant to be copied literally. Rather it is offered as a resource, some ideas to stir one's own thinking, a glimpse of something satisfying and transforming that can happen when a group of people take their ritualizing seriously. The work continues to be experimental. No one presumes that everything works all the time. In fact, perfection, as a norm, is the least of our concerns. Ongoing human life with all its imperfections intimately connected to something beyond what we know—this is what we celebrate.

The examples below are not familiar forms based on institutional liturgies. Though liturgies characterized as feminist include both familiar forms, as well as emerging ones, more often than not the planners of feminist liturgies experiment with the forms and content to evaluate all aspects of liturgical expressions. Symbols, texts, and sounds are drawn from various traditions.

One frequently asked question about feminist liturgies is whether what we do is liturgy or group therapy. Typical understandings of liturgy as glorification of God and the sanctification of people, for some people, are difficult to apply. While it is certainly true that, like therapy, in feminist liturgies we intend to face the truths of our lives, there is another level of our interaction as well. Unlike therapy we intentionally do this work in light of our relationships with God. We draw strength from traditions of faith, including what has been lost, layers of interpretations and information we regularly search for and add. We expect God among us, with us, around us. We cherish the invitation of holiness inherent in worship and especially holiness that blesses imperfection, the chance to begin again and again. Feminist liturgies do not avoid the praise of God; we praise God through all of our experiences, rather than the limited expressions handed on to us.

What follows are *three* liturgies of a public character engaging rather large groups of both women and men and *three* of a more intimate nature with relatively small groups, two with women only, one with both men and women. Though everything that was planned is not reproduced here, the liturgies are described in some detail and in the present tense so that the reader may experience a sense of immediacy. The following chapter gives attention to the planning of feminist liturgy to show how our "learnings" can be applied to traditional weekly institutional worship and to liturgies outside institutional structures.

A. Women Expecting . . . An Advent Experience[1]

One of the most challenging aspects within the process of shaping feminist liturgies is to address the times of the year in which there are powerful memories of particular ways of celebrating certain feasts. Such times include Easter, Christmas, Yom Kippur, Rosh Ha Shanah, and Passover. The following liturgy was designed to mark Advent, through a different path.

It was organized by the New York Women's Liturgy Group. After six years of gathering monthly as a small group of women, we planned this liturgy for friends and family to widen the circle of our ritual experiences. One hundred and fifty people joined us. The

---

[1] The text of this liturgy and the one on the "Afterlife" are part of a packet of liturgies prepared by Claire S. Derway, samples of the work of the New York Women's Liturgy Group, 1120 Fifth Ave., New York, N.Y. 10128. The planners of the liturgy were members of the New York Women's Liturgy Group.

liturgy took place in a large, renovated neo-Gothic chapel with typical rectangular dimensions.

PEOPLE enter through an antechamber modeled on a stereotypical church: pews in rows, darkly-lit, a hymnal on every chair, a pulpit, a handsomely-bound Bible, a cross, and an altar on which there are two candles. As they come out of this space, they discover a warmly-lighted circular space, with four painted panels on its periphery that suggest rooms of an apartment. Furniture in the center of the circle continues this impression. As people come in, they are given cups of warm cider. They mill around freely, eventually taking a place in a circular arrangement of chairs where they find a song sheet.

On a rug in the central space is a table with four candles on it. A member of the New York Women's Liturgy Group lights the candles one by one and welcomes everyone to this liturgy:

MEMBER:　　We are delighted to have all of you here with us today to celebrate an Advent experience. We are here because we are expecting something different—of ourselves, of our world, of our relationship with God.

　　　　　　The Advent season emphasizes expectation. The history of the season is long and rich. We want to mingle our histories with it. We want to recover stories that have been lost through neglect, through indifference, and through oversight. We want to reclaim that which is ours.

Then follows a reading of a revised genealogy of Matthew's Gospel prepared by Ann Patrick Ware. It is read by FOUR WOMEN, a NARRATOR, and the CONGREGATION who are instructed to repeat the same phrase throughout the reading:

NARRATOR:　A different genealogy of Jesus Christ, the son of Miriam, the daughter of Anna:

FIRST READER:
　　　　　　Sarah was the mother of Isaac
　　　　　　Rebekah was the mother of Jacob
　　　　　　Leah was the mother of Judah
　　　　　　Tamar was the mother of Perez.
　　　　　　The names of the mothers of Hezron, Ram,
　　　　　　Amminadab, Nashon, and Salmon have been lost.

NARRATOR: The names of the mothers have been lost.

CONGREGATION: The names of the mothers have been lost.

The pattern of tracing the genealogy though the names of the mothers continues to this closing:

NARRATOR: The sum of generations is therefore:
fourteen from Sarah to David's mother;
fourteen from Bathsheba to the Babylonian
deportation to Miriam,
the mother of Jesus who is called the Christ.

A DANCER enters the center of the space. Humming "Lo How A Rose E'er Blooming," a fifteenth-century carol that presents the rose as a symbol of Mary or for Christ, she interprets the traditional words of the text as they are sung, accompanied by a flute. Then follows a modern genealogy:

READERS *(dividing the material among them):*
The generations of women from Miriam, called Mary, the mother of Jesus, continue to this day.

Women like Dolores Huerta, the mother of twelve children and the vice president of the United Farm Workers. Today Dolores Huerta heads a campaign to alert the public to the effects of pesticides upon all of us.

Women like Joyce Mary Horner, a twentieth-century woman who taught English at Mount Holyoke College until she entered a nursing home at age seventy. There she faced her own impending death but she also claimed her power to act on her concerns for other people in the home. Horner became an interpreter and advocate for them.

Women like Rebecca Cox Jackson, a nineteenth-century freeborn black woman—a preacher, healer, prophet and religious visionary. She called upon God, her loving Mother, a friend to all the poor and helpless.

EVERYONE sings the traditional chant melody "O Come, O Come Emmanuel," with an adapted text, the first of a number of stanzas to be sung throughout the liturgy:

ALL *(singing):*
>This holy season teaches us that we
>Who now, with Christ, share one humanity,
>Must do our best to bring this fragile earth
>Into the peace that heralds a new birth.
>Rejoice, rejoice! Our freedom is at hand.
>The Dawn of Justice shines upon the land.

The next section of the service, the heart of it, includes congregational movement, singing, and listening:

MEMBER: It takes a lot of interrupted movement to go from past to present, a lot of interrupted effort to push out into new and unexplored possibilities. Sometimes we lose our footing. Sometimes it takes our whole being to make one small struggling step forward. Sometimes we can make a mighty leap. Sometimes we stumble, we bump into one another. Sometimes we soar. But all the time we are on the way.

We do move individually and collectively. This afternoon, even though we are barely able to sit comfortably (there are so many of us), we are going to try to move comfortably as a whole group and then stop and be attentive. And we are going to have some help.

With the action modeled by a DANCER, the WHOLE GROUP walks rhythmically in a prescribed series of steps singing:

ALL *(singing):*
>Walker, walker, there is no road.
>Walker, walker, there is no road.
>The road is made by walking.[2]

As we move and sing, TWO WOMEN read.

WOMAN 1:   We are expectant, ripe for the delivery of newness.

ALL *(singing and moving in rhythm):*
>Walker, walker, there is no road.

---

[2] Text: Antonio Machado, trans. from the Spanish by Ada Maria Isasi-Diaz, a member of the Women's Liturgy Group. Tune: Annette T. Covatta.

Walker, walker, there is no road.
The road is made by walking.

WOMAN 2: Elbow deep in the stuff of life, we expect to spend our creativity making home on earth.

ALL *(singing and moving in rhythm):*
Walker, walker, there is no road.
Walker, walker, there is no road.
The road is made by walking.

WOMAN 1: We expect to be afraid, but to find the courage to walk away from places that are secure but deadening.

ALL *(singing and moving in rhythm):*
Walker, walker, there is no road.
Walker, walker, there is no road.
The road is made by walking.

WOMAN 2: Expectation heralds the prospects in our lives. Expectation lives by gracious insistence. Expectation is sweet flowing courage: Adventure! Expectation is Advent.

ALL *(singing and moving in rhythm):*
Walker, walker, there is no road.
Walker, walker, there is no road.
The road is made by walking.

Then follows a time of personal silence in which ALL are invited to remember our own genealogy and then to speak with one or two neighboring persons about our expectations of this Advent season. From our speaking we are invited to act, first lighting a candle, naming our matrilineal heritage, and then in spontaneous fashion calling out our expectations of ourselves, our world and our God. The liturgy closes with a reading of a poem by May Sarton:

READER: The earth feels old tonight
And we who live and stand on the cold rim
Face a new year.
It is raining everywhere.
As if the rain were mercy
As if the rain were peace.
Peace falling on our hair.

Open your hearts tonight; let them burn!
Let them light a way in the dark.
Let them one by one affirm
There is hope for a staff:
I say it will flower in our hands.
We shall go garlanded.
There is the fine fresh stuff of faith for a coat:
We shall go warm.
We shall go on by the light of our hearts.
We shall burn mightily in the new year.
We shall go on together—
O you who stand alone on the rim of the earth
    and are cold,
I salute you here.[3]

ALL sing an adapted version of "Carol of the Advent" sung to the tune of
"Joy to the World."

Look to the East
The time is near:
The crowning of the year.
Come, make your house all fair and bright
And ready for the holy night.
Put strife and woe away,
Run to greet this Christmas Day
For Love, the Guest, is on the way.[4]

The chapel ceiling opens and rose petals, glitter, and bits of evergreen and
boxwood are released to grace all present. The evening concludes with re-
freshments.

WHY IS THIS LITURGY FEMINIST?

1. The celebration of an ancient tradition evoked a fresh layer of
meanings. We discovered them not through discussion but by doing
something other than what we had inherited. We rewrote texts,
added new ones, incorporated a broad variety of symbols and added
movements that expressed a path full of surprises, anchored in hope.

[3] "Greeting, New Year's Eve 1937," in *Selected Poems of May Sarton*, ed.
Serena Sue Hilsinger and Lois Byrnes (W. W. Norton & Co., 1978) 68.
[4] Adapted for this occasion by Ann Patrick Ware.

2. We named those women who had been neglected, forgotten and even lost—those foremothers in religious and secular and personal history as well as contemporary stories of women struggling for justice. Identifying their stories and knowing them gives authority and strength to our own journeys. We claimed it.

3. We used sounds and texts, ancient and modern, received, and our own.

4. Words rewritten for the tune "O Come, O Come Emmanuel" reminded us of our accountability to each other, a significant characteristic of feminist liturgy. Our fragile earth community needs a new birth. It will come forth through us in our everyday lives.

5. The Holy One was called upon as "The Dawn of Justice," a title appropriate for a liturgy that confidently respects the freedom of God. It is a name for God that expresses our quest for justice as feminists.

6. The organization of the space represented our journey and history from institution to home to a reshaped public space, from invisibility and disempowerment to a public voice with strength and authority.

7. We used our bodies as resources of insight and action. We moved together to symbolize that there is no road except the one we pave together.

8. Though the group was large, there were varied ways for everyone to participate. We expected active participation, though not necessarily the same type for everyone. Collaborative liturgical work is essential to our collective wisdom.

9. The experience was serious, but it was also fun. Play is an important ingredient in good liturgy. Play provides encouragement to let go of defenses and absorb, or in some cases, reject what is happening.

B. *When Madness Comes Home*[5]

Madness, depression and any form of mental illness scare all of us. Mental illness conjures up feelings of guilt, helplessness, frustration, loss, and anger. For some of us, it is deemed the epitome of loss of control. People with mental illness, some helped by medicine and therapy, others not helped at all, are in our midst. While many families confront the vagaries of mental illness, they often find it difficult to talk about its realities.

[5] Victoria Secunda, *When Madness Comes Home: Help and Hope for the Children, Siblings, and Partners of the Mentally Ill* (New York: Hyperion, 1997).

The following liturgy brings together the resources of Judaism and the support of a community upon the death of a family member who was mentally ill.[6] It seeks not only to offer solace and understanding to the family of the person who has died but to connect the resources of Judaism with the anguish of dealing with mental illness.

1. Prayer and Study

MEMBERS of the Beth Am congregation gather in a home to remember the sister of Miriam Frank who had died of breast cancer, but had been mentally ill her entire adult life.

The liturgy begins with the singing of "Hine Ma Tov"("How good and sweet it is for brother/sisters to sit together"), portions from When Madness Comes Home *and Psalm 88 (all read by individuals who have had some intimate relationship to mental illness.) Two brief excerpts:*

READER: I remember very vividly the last day she lived at home. She went berserk at the breakfast table with my father. . . . But I had to go to school. So I went into the hall to get the elevator, and stood streaming with tears, because there was nobody who could comfort me.[7]

READER: My soul was just destroyed by my daughter's illness. . . . For many years I blamed myself and withdrew from everyone, because I couldn't bear the pain. I even fired God.[8]

READER: *Psalm 88*
O God of my deliverance,
when I cry out in the night before you
let my prayer reach You;

[Why] does your fury fall heavy upon me? . . .
[Why] do You make my companions shun me?

---

[6] The service was prepared by Rabbi Margaret Moers Wenig and Dr. Miriam Frank, Beth Am, The People's Temple, New York, N.Y., June 1997. It includes both prayer and study, a combination familiar to Jews. The translations of the psalms in this liturgy were excerpts from varied sources including Rabbi Wenig's own translations.

[7] Secunda, 49–50.

[8] Secunda, 123.

I am shut in and cannot go out.
My eyes pine away from affliction.
I call to You, O God, each day;
I stretch out my hands to You.

From my youth I have been afflicted and near death.
I suffer Your terrors, I am numb.
Your wrath overwhelms me;
Your terrors destroy me. . . .
You have distanced lover and neighbor from me.
Those who know me are in darkness.

The community offers a blessing for the Torah study. Then follows a series of eight traditional texts, chosen to reflect Jewish thought about various kinds of disabilities. Interspersed near the end are two excerpts from When Madness Comes Home. *After each reading, the MEMBERS of the community discuss the text. Here is an excerpted section:*

READER: Who is *shoteh*? (imbecile, insane)
            One who goes out alone at night, and walks about in
            the cemetery, and one who tears his[9] clothes, and one
            who destroys what has been given to him.

            Tosefta, Terumot 1:3

READER: Neither the purchase nor the sale of [i.e., by] *[shoteh]*
            an imbecile is valid, nor are his gifts valid. The court
            appoints an administrator for imbeciles as it does for
            minors.

            The *Mishnah Torah* of Maimonides: Sacrifices,
            Pilgrim Offering 2:1

READER: It is harmful [sic] to clash with a deaf-mute, an imbecile
            [shoteh], or a minor; if a man injures one of these he is
            held liable; if they injure other people, they are exempt.
            . . .[10]

            The *Mishnah Torah* of Maimonides: Damages,
            Assault and Battery 4:20

[9] These ancient Jewish texts refer only to men.

[10] The texts from "Damages, Assault and Battery" set up a confusing situation. Is a *shotel* considered to be other than human? The reading generated a lengthy discussion.

READER: I guess I just snapped, because nothing I did made any difference. I said to [my schizophrenic brother], "That's it. You're on your own. . . . I am finished with you." Well, within twenty-four hours he got himself into treatment. . . . I really look forward to seeing him now, because he's helping himself.[11]

When Madness Comes Home

Then the leader offers traditional prayers for the sick and their families, as well as bedtime prayers asking for a peaceful night's rest, interspersed with readings from When Madness Comes Home. *The readings touch on the multiple aspects of dealing with mental illness in a family: the implications for other members' emotional development, the need to protect the mentally ill, and the necessity to go beyond the family for help. I am including only one example of the five pairings:*

READER: My greatest fear was that what happened to my mother would happen to me . . . I didn't have any friends because I was afraid that if people got to know me, they'd see the flaws in my character and lock me away . . . . The one place I could allow myself to have emotions was a big rock in the woods. I would go to that rock and try to get in touch with the anger and the pain. It reached a point that I invented a woman who, in my mind, would walk up the trail and sit beside me on the rock and talk with me. She'd put her arm around me and say, "I care what's happening to you." I went to that rock every chance I got.[12]

When Madness Comes Home

READER: *Psalm 121*
I will lift up my eyes to the hills—
from whence shall my help come?

My help comes from God,
Creator of heaven and earth. . . .

God will protect you through all evil.
God will protect your soul.

[11] Secunda, 269.
[12] Secunda, 144.

God will watch over your going out and your coming in from this time forth, and for evermore.

2. Memorial Service

The context for remembering a woman who lived her entire adult life with mental illness is set. Now we remember her particularly in the memorial liturgy. MIRIAM speaks about her sister, after which the rest of the COMMUNITY responds.

ALL: *Zichrona livracha.* May her memory be a blessing.

READER: From "Kaddish for Naomi Ginsberg 1894–1956" by Allen Ginsberg. An excerpt from Section I:

There. Rest. No more suffering for you. I know where you've gone, it's good.

All the accumulation of life, that wear us out—clocks, bodies—consciousness, shoes, breasts—begotten sons—
your Communism—"Paranoia" into hospitals . . .

This is the end, the redemption from Wilderness, way for the Wonderer, House sought for All, black handkerchief washed clean by weeping—page beyond Psalm—Last change of mine and Naomi—to God's perfect Darkness—Death, stay thy phantoms!

The CONGREGATION interrupts the Kaddish singing "El Moley Rachamin" (a prayer that Miriam's sister might finally find peace under the wings of God's presence). Ginsberg's "Kaddish" (excerpted) continues.

READER: In the world which He has created according to His will Blessed Praised. . . . In the house in Newark Blessed is He! In the madhouse Blessed is He! In the house of Death Blessed is He! . . .

Blessed be you Naomi in tears! Blessed be you Naomi in fears!
Blessed Blessed Blessed in sickness! . . .

The memorial liturgy ends with ALL reciting the traditional "Mourner's Kaddish," after which comes this excerpt from When Madness Comes Home:

READER: Recovery . . . is based upon the empowerment of the
            survivor and the creation of new connections. Recov-
            ery can take place only within the context of relation-
            ships; it cannot occur in isolation.[13]

*Then ALL sing a reprise from the beginning, "Hine Ma Tov," a simple, fa-
miliar, chant-like round.*

WHY IS THIS LITURGY FEMINIST?

1. The experience broke the silence associated with mental illness. Though mental illness, in a variety of manifestations, is widespread among us, it is rarely mentioned in our institutional liturgies.
All of us, those who are mentally ill and those who are not, share
many of the same feelings: we're afraid, we're ashamed, we're angry,
we feel God has deserted us, we're not sure whom to blame and we
feel responsible, yet at times we cannot sustain responsibility. In this
liturgy speech substituted for silence; what had been invisible was
claimed. The liturgy expressed compassion, as well as freedom. For
some moments, the community felt relief from fear, shame, and em-
barrassment and, in their place, came rest, comfort, togetherness,
and blessing.

2. The texts from Jewish traditions were used honestly. Some
comforted, some surprised, some discomforted. Many people felt
relieved to know that Judaism supported their secret, profound feelings of fear, loneliness, despair. At the same time people were
troubled upon realizing that the texts about mentally ill persons im-
plied mentally ill people were not quite human. Like all women,
they were considered outside the law.

3. A mix of traditional resources and contemporary texts was
used to urge individual and community responses.

4. God was named through a variety of expressions, both female
and male. The latter was suggested in the juxtaposition of *When
Madness Comes Home* with Psalm 121. The God of the psalm is like
the woman in the text who says, "I care what's happening to you."

5. The planning was collaborative. Rabbi Maggie Wenig and Dr.
Miriam Frank researched the material and prepared the form following the traditional combination of study and prayer.

---

[13] Judith Lewis Herman, *Trauma and Recovery,* as cited in Victoria Secunda,
When Madness Comes Home, 286.

6. The participation was reciprocal and relational. People who had experienced mental illness themselves or knew it in their families read the texts. There was time to speak, to be silent, to claim harsh realities and to feel support. The liturgy generated a spectrum of questions and feelings.

7. There was room for strong, ignored feelings, even outrage directed to God, along with the traditional expectation of the blessing of God.

8. Though the goals of the liturgy included comfort for the mourners, it also intended to provide an experience of redemption found in Jewish resources, sought after, put together and offered in a community setting.

9. As stated in the last excerpt from *When Madness Comes Home*, the liturgy *enacted* what the words and songs suggested: recovery requires relationships. This community came together as Jews to draw from Jewish traditions and other experiences. They needed strength from each other to live with more confidence and peace. The ritualizing enabled them to bond as Jews and as people who knew intimately the struggles of mental illness and to claim varying relationships with God. It was an act of redemption, of justice.

C. A Ritual of Healing from Childhood Sexual Abuse

Sexual violence is a subject that is never distant from feminist liturgies. Sexual violence is one of the most egregious expressions of sexism and male dominance. When women gather to remember and imagine what is true in their relationships, inevitably some will speak about personal experiences of sexual abuse.

What follows is a ritual planned by a woman, Carol,[14] who was regularly molested by her father, beginning at age four and continuing through her adolescence. Carol's father, a psychiatrist, came into her room at night, forced his penis in her mouth and lifted her nightdress to touch her small body. When he finished, he hypnotized her so she would forget what had happened. Carol's family and friends came to know her as a morose child. Although her father knew the reason for this behavior, he never did anything to alter this assumption.[15]

[14] The names of the participants in this ritual have been changed.
[15] Notes from one of the participants in the ritual.

Carol chose nighttime at the beach for the ritualizing and brought two symbols of her experiences of abuse: a pink cloth to signify the pink nightdress she wore as a child and a cord of blue and white wool to represent the bathrobe belt her father put around her neck when abusing her. Carol invited a small group of five people (friends, a survivor of sexual abuse and her therapist) to be with her. She needed this community, people who understood the realities of this abuse. Carol looked to them to make "sacred space" for her and for themselves, the experience of freedom and hope where she could dare to imagine an end to the remembering and the feelings that continued to strangle her. The group called upon God, expected God's intimate presence among them. The ritual includes praying, singing, moving, and speaking.

FIVE PEOPLE gather at the beach in silence and sit in a circle around a fire. A reading of Psalm 27 *breaks the silence.*

READER: The LORD is my light and my salvation;
        whom shall I fear?
    The LORD is the stronghold of my life;
        of whom shall I be afraid?

    When evildoers assail me
        to devour my flesh—
    my adversaries and foes—
        they shall stumble and fall. . . .

    I believe that I shall see the goodness of the LORD
        in the land of the living.
    Wait for the LORD;
        Be strong, and let your heart take courage;
    Wait for the LORD!

EACH PERSON is invited to visualize Carol as a small child by drawing a picture of her. It is an opportunity to symbolize the loss of childhood. Carol draws a child under a menacing cloud. Another draws a child with the words "image of God," written on a heart. Each reflects aloud on the picture she/he draws and then burns it, to set the image free and to restore a redeemed image of Carol. It is a time for remembering and imagining.

    Then there is a time for praying words that speak of abuse, violence, and a God who would be faithful in the midst of powerlessness. It is a time for singing sounds of the ranting and raving of demons and a plea for freedom.[16]

Now, Carol tells her own story. As she recalls the facts and memories of her abuse, she feeds the pink material and the cord into the fire. When she finishes, one person fills a bucket with water, sea water with healing salt. Each person passes it to another for a cleansing action: washing of tears, purging from experience, whatever each one needs. Many people touch Carol with the water. The cleansing is not only for Carol but for all others, too.

Each person is invited to search the beach for a symbol to give Carol, as a reminder of their support for her journey ahead (e.g., a stone; a flower; a piece of glass, once sharp and dangerous, now worn, smooth and safe). As each presents it, they all listen to the singing of Louis Rose's "Blackbird singing in the dead of night, Take these broken wings and learn to fly."

The liturgy closes with Carol's reflection about the importance of this ritual. The fire is extinguished and Carol and her friends walk together back to the house on the beach, all the while singing "Amazing Grace."

WHY IS THIS LITURGY FEMINIST?

1. The liturgy named the sin of sexual abuse, a reality many women and children face daily, but one rarely mentioned in institutional liturgies.

2. The liturgy did not avoid the *terror* of sexual abuse. Through visceral objects, sounds, words, the community acknowledged its presence. Nothing was "made nice."

3. The ambiguity of the divine was named: one who will protect, but one who also may not.

4. The space was particularly chosen and shaped to be a resource for healing and comfort.

5. The process of claiming, of cleansing, of transforming, of remembering destructive relationships and of imagining redeemed relationships was enacted with determination and freedom. It empowered Carol and others as well. Though this ritualizing was initiated because of Carol's experiences, it did not stop there, but rather drew out a spectrum of human experiences from everyone who gathered.

6. The liturgy expected healing, at least a step toward it, healing in the context of faith, in a context of questions about how God is

---

[16] The hymn "Silence! Frenzied, Unclean Spirit" by Carol Doran (tune) and Thomas H. Troeger (text) can be found in many hymnals, including *The New Century Hymnal* (Cleveland: Pilgrim Press, 1995) no. 176.

with us. The liturgy was an experience of the freedom God promises, a freedom known in traces for sure, but tasted and felt when a community like this one comes together to embody it.

7. The liturgy named and cast out evil, inspiring resistance. It was an act of justice.

D. A Memorial Liturgy

What happens after death? Artists offer images, writers interpret ancient texts, scholars suggest possible scenarios. But no one really knows. We can only guess. The guessing seems more urgent after the death of someone we love. Is there any continuing relationship? And if so, of what kind, we wonder. Or as my niece Katharine once put it after the death of her grandfather: "Does he know he is dead?"[17]

This memorial liturgy was designed to remember a father and a brother of two members of a women's liturgy group. The focus, at the request of one of the bereaved members, was "the afterlife." The planners did not propose to discuss the afterlife but rather through the ritualizing, to provide an opportunity to discover insights about living their own lives differently precisely because we cannot imagine what the afterlife will be. Perhaps we will be surprised or perhaps disappointed, overjoyed or overwhelmed. We don't know.

The liturgy has a simple setting and form. A GROUP OF TWELVE WOMEN gather around a table in the living room of one of the member's homes. On the table are burning candles, long-standing symbols of life, and pictures of loved ones who had died, relatives of each of the women. After a brief introduction to set the framework and tone of the liturgy, we listen to a reading of "Meeting the Dead" by Alicia Ostriker. Here are some excerpts:

READER: If we've loved them, it's what we want, and sometimes
Wanting works. With my father it happened driving
From Santa Monica to Pasadena
A night of full moon, the freeway wide
Open, the palm trees black. I was recalling
how for two years after that shy man's death
I thought only of death, how in April weather
I used to lock the Volkswagen windows so nothing
Pleasant or fragrant would reach me . . .

[17] Words of Katharine Walton, age 7.

. . . I hated it
That we would never meet in mutual old
Age to drink a beer—it was all he ever
Drank—and declare our love, the way I'd planned
All through high school, picturing us in
A sunny doorway facing a back garden;
Something out of a book.

This has been mourning, I thought; then a sound came
Like a door clicking closed, and I understood
Right off that I was finished, that I would
Never feel any more grief for him—
And at the same time he was present; had been
I now saw, all along, for these twelve years,
Waiting for me to finish my mourning.[18]

Why? Why such grieving? Why pain? Why? ONE OF THE LEADERS begins a reflection on "why":

LEADER: In general we take life for granted. We live in a series of absorbing activities, sometimes routine, sometimes challenging, but usually we are busy with life's requirements, until we are reminded of our own mortality, perhaps by the death of one we love or by confronting personal limitations. The reminder is at best a rude interruption asking us to pay attention to the question "why?" . . .[19]

Then comes an introduction to a reading.

LEADER: It happens that a people, a nation, a race have to grapple with why, in conditions which are inhuman, in God-awful circumstances. In the horror of human brutality, someone has the courage to ask, "Why?" More, someone has the inner resources to shape a response. Etty Hillesum, a twenty-seven-year-old Jewish woman, lived in Amsterdam and kept a journal from 1941–1942,

---

[18] Alicia Ostriker, "Meeting the Dead" in *Early Ripening: American Women's Poetry Now*, ed. Marge Piercy (New York: Pandora Press, 1987) 180.

[19] These words were written by Eileen King, one of the planners of the liturgy.

years of genocide. She offers her attempts at a response to why.

Various MEMBERS of the group read excerpts from Etty Hillesum's journal.[20]

READER: How is it that this stretch of heathland surrounded by barbed wire, through which so much misery has flooded, nevertheless remains inscribed in my memory as something almost lovely? How is it that my spirit, far from being oppressed, seemed to grow lighter and brighter there? It is because I read the signs of the times and they did not seem meaningless to me. Surrounded by my writers and my poets and the flowers on my desk I loved life. And there among the barracks, full of haunted and persecuted people I found confirmation of my love of life . . . .

READER: Most people here are much worse than they need be because they write off their longing for friends and family as so many losses in their lives, when they count the fact that their heart is able to long so hard and to love so much among their great blessings.

READER: People sometimes say, "You must try to make the best of things." I find this such a feeble thing to say. Everywhere things are both good and bad at the same time. . . . "Making the best of things" is a nauseating expression, and so is "seeing the good in everything."

READER: My life has become an uninterrupted dialogue with You, O God, one great dialogue.

We listen to the verses and ALL sing the chorus of "Is That All There Is?"[21] *a song made famous by Peggy Lee. An excerpt:*

READER: I remember when I was a very little girl . . . our house caught on fire . . . I'll never forget my father's face as

[20] Etty Hillesum, *An Interrupted Life: The Diaries of Etty Hillesum 1941–43,* English trans. by Arnold J. Pomerans (New York: Henry Holt Publishing Co., 1996) 209, 327–38, 332.

[21] "Is That All There Is?" by Jerry Leiber and Mike Stoller.

he gathered me up in his arms and raced through the burning building onto the pavement. I stood there shivering in my pajamas . . . and watched the whole world go up in flames . . . And when it was over . . . I said to myself, "Is that all there is to a fire?"

ALL sing the chorus.

ALL *(singing):*
> IS THAT ALL THERE IS?
> IS THAT ALL THERE IS?
> If that's all there is, my friends, then let's keep dancing
> Let's break out the booze and have a ball
> If that's all there is.

The question posed in the song becomes the question for group reflection. "No treatise needed," suggests the leader. "Instead, think of this WHY (the After-life) as sneaking up on you. You momentarily need to regain your footing. What shape did the question take, and what did you learn in your response?"

In the quiet time for us to gather our thoughts, we listen to a section of "Quartets for the End of Time" by Olivier Messaien, haunting, mysterious, generous music, sounds of an image of God present in the midst of death. Then one by one, we share our responses to the question.

The liturgy closes with a tangible reminder that we don't know. We only guess. From under the table, to our surprise and delight, comes a basket we had not seen earlier. In it are gaily wrapped presents for each person.

ALL follow this with a spontaneous rendering of "The Best of Times Is Now" from "La Cage aux Folles" by Jerry Herman. It reminds us to notice the power of these moments.

WHY IS THIS LITURGY FEMINIST?

1. Our ritualizing was an organic experience. Its focus came from ordinary questions lived out in our day-to-day lives. Death leaves in its wake profound questions and mixed feelings. Funerals come and go, but these unanswered questions persist. We gathered to support our friends in mourning by joining them in a quest for insight and perhaps healing and transformation through ritualizing. We came together to pay attention to the rhythm of death and life in the ordinary course of things.

2. Resources were not limited to canonized texts nor to hack-neyed, or even regularly heard words or sounds that float over us.

But rather, they included poignant and at times humorous expressions of what is common in everyone's life: yearning, asking why, letting go, weeping, continuing on. Things that encouraged a breadth of thinking and speaking from the mind and heart, whatever could make fresh connections, ancient and new, were incorporated.

3. Likewise, there was a variety of ways to invoke or encounter the presence of the Holy One. In this liturgy only in the Hillesum reading was the name "God" actually uttered. However, the planners chose the Messaien music for its hints about the presence of God in the midst of the mysteries of the end of time. The reflections which participants offered on the Afterlife also included descriptions about relationships with God.

4. The success of this liturgy depended on each person's participation. The most important moments of a feminist liturgy are the occasions when each person has the opportunity to say what she is feeling or thinking in response to the ritual actions. One comment often influences everyone else's experience. The comments were rich, surprising, moving, and comforting.

5. The liturgy did not end with an answer to the question why. No one expected it. It was a time and a space when something unpredictable happened, something about grace was embodied, something transforming was felt and known.

6. The environment honored women and drew upon our capacity to remember relationships and to imagine an afterlife that empowered our everyday relationships.

E. Ritual after a Mastectomy

Breast cancer is frightening. At worst, a woman faces the prospect of death. At best, her survival always requires some physical change, at times as radical as a mastectomy, not an attractive solution in a society that prizes a perfect female body.

The following ritual was planned when, active in the New York Women's Liturgy Group, I returned home after a bilateral mastectomy. The setting was a member's home.

ONE OF THE MEMBERS *begins the ritual.*

MEMBER: We're here because our friend has just had a mastectomy. We want to support her and help speed her recovery. We want to bless her so that her healing will be complete and as easy as possible.[22]

Then follows a reading from Adrienne Rich[23] that reminds us that we do not need experts to tell us about our lives. We know what is true and what is urgent. We can name our pain, our hope, and our questions. What we need are opportunities to remember, claim, and affirm what we know. What we need is to listen to ourselves and to trust what we hear.

A MEMBER instructs the group.

MEMBER: Let's consider for a few minutes that deeply innate, merely physical life that surges through us in our bloodstream. It is hidden, unseen, needs no tending to on our part by voluntary attention, and it is the very course and stuff of life.

Take a minute now to find your own pulse. Now help your neighbor to the left to touch yours, and let us sit for a moment in a circle of life, in touch with another's pulse, joined, silent, throbbing.

Now that all have felt the networking of our life, ONE OF THE GROUP puts a rebozo, a large, soft, purple shawl made by women in Guatemala, a "mantle of caring," around me. A MEMBER offers a personal word to me.

MEMBER: In addition to the wish we have to unite our life with yours, we want to say in what admiration we hold you. You are a model of what it means to assume responsibility for tough decisions. We admire the way you let us into your crisis. You didn't shut us out as though it were not important to us or as though we needed to be spared. We admire the way you understood—or tried to understand what your own needs would be: your need not to be fussed over, your need for privacy, your understanding that you might require help and that you would ask for it. And we want to testify that by your careful attention and pain in making a decision

---

[22] All readers were members of the New York Women's Liturgy Group.

[23] Adrienne Rich, *On Lies, Secrets, and Silence: Selected Prose 1966–1978* (New York: W. W. Norton, 1979).

in the few options open to you, you helped us all learn more about responsibility, maturing suffering, about our relationship to our bodies, and what we can be to one another. So we salute you tonight.

Another reading by Adrienne Rich[24] expresses well what we want to say to you. In it the members of the Women's Liturgy Group remind Janet (and themselves) to refuse to be silent while others speak in our name. Responsibility to ourselves requires us to claim our minds, to respect our bodies as inestimable treasures of particular and distinctive knowing. Responsibility to ourselves compels us to reject relationships in which we are treated as objects.

Another MEMBER speaks.

MEMBER: But taking responsibility for oneself is not without cost. We can't even name the cost for another (sometimes cannot even do it for ourselves); can't name it for Janet. It's part of her hidden life, and we are not asking her to recount it.

But we will try to name some costs we ourselves have paid or how we understand being responsible for ourselves and the price it demands.

ALL share some silent time for reflection.
    Then there is a "swapping of costs": EACH PERSON describes a moment in her own life when taking responsibility cost something, e.g., when speaking rather than being silent changed a relationship or challenged a job, when recognition of a destructive behavior required leaving what was comfortable.
    To conclude, EACH MEMBER of the community is invited to bless Janet: to touch a part of her body and bless it with her own words and gesture.
    ALL sing the "Song of the Soul" by Cris Williamson, a familiar song that expresses hope and healing, to conclude the liturgy.

WHY IS THIS LITURGY FEMINIST?

1. Words about breasts are avoided in most institutional worship. Though breasts are a part of nurturing, mothering, interdependence, beauty, and sexual pleasure—all important aspects of human life—

24 Ibid.

a mention of a woman's breasts is most often off limits. This liturgy acknowledged the loss of a breast and the changes a mastectomy demands.

2. For most survivors, breast cancer involves recovery with a cost. With honesty, solidarity, and affection the women gathered to face these realities for the woman involved and for themselves.

3. No one named an experience for someone else as if anyone else could know. We each spoke for ourselves.

4. Solidarity was expressed physically as well as verbally, body to body, pulse to pulse.

5. The loss of a breast has both physical and emotional ramifications. Both were addressed in the blessing and the readings.

6. The loss of any body part affects the whole. The blessing was not directed to the missing breasts but to other parts of the body still capable, still beautiful, still healthy.

7. Healing requires self-affirmation. The group articulated its own testimony of the significance of this particular woman's life to encourage her own self-affirmation.

8. The liturgy was for everyone. Though it was clearly planned for a particular person, each person named the cost of taking responsibility in her own life. This sharing was mutually empowering.

F. A Halloween Service: Celebrating Sophia in Our Wise Older Women

Halloween is traditionally a time for fantasy: festivity and fright, ghosts and goblins, masks, costumes and parades. At the midpoint between the autumn solstice and the winter solstice, for a short time, we live between the worlds of the dead and living. We dress up, trying on the characteristics of a saint or a favorite personality; we pretend to be an animal or an imagined being of varying sorts. It is a time for fun, celebration and remembering.

According to Celtic legend[25] this season, called "Samhain," also offered an opportunity to honor the elderly: grandparents and aging relatives. For this liturgy we decided to combine two traditions: aspects of Halloween and a tribute to older women. The

[25] Zsuzsannna E. Budapest, *The Grandmother of Time: A Woman's Book of Celebrations, Spells, and Sacred Objects for Every Month of the Year* (San Francisco: Harper & Row, 1979) 208.

liturgy is a feast of wisdom, particularly, God's wisdom revealed in wise women.

This liturgy stretched what most religious traditions express about God in relation to ourselves. The older women who collaborated in the planning of it and who led the liturgy were quite surprised themselves. At first it was startling to imagine using images of God as an aged crone, as a witch, as Sophia, a female face of God. However, as they continued to talk about the images and especially when they experienced them in the liturgy, they realized that these were words about them, words usually used negatively as dismissive words about women. In this liturgy they and the community were invited to know God through images of women with wrinkled bodies, through older women who are wise from long years of struggle, a wisdom that heals and comforts and dares. While they knew that some in the congregation might also have reservations and experience some resistance at first, these women confidently believed that the beauty, truth, and holiness inherent in the liturgy would overcome fear and reluctance. They were right.

The liturgy is organized around three actions: women gossiping, witches stirring a brew, and a crone spinning her story. Women prepared and led the service; the participants included both men and women.

As PEOPLE come into the chapel, MEMBERS of the community welcome each person and give them a printed worship aid. The liturgy begins with a prelude, sung by a SOLOIST, an adaptation of the song "I'm Still Here" by Steven Sondheim, adapted by Ann Patrick Ware.

TWO READERS invite ALL to Wisdom's Feast.[26]

READERS *(alternating paragraphs):*

> This is a liturgical tradition inspired by the figure of Wisdom—Sophia—a rare female face of God found in the Hebrew Scriptures, in the books of Wisdom and of Proverbs. The early Church looked to the Wisdom tra-

[26] These words of welcome were written by Susan Blain who together with Janet Walton conceived and led the planning of the service. The work of Susan Cady, Marian Ronan, and Hal Taussig in *Wisdom's Feast* guided us and provided varied resources for this liturgy (San Francisco: Harper & Row, 1989).

ditions to help them understand who Jesus was: "image of the unseen God," Firstborn of Creation in whom all things were created—Jesus, wisdom, Sophia. Wisdom builds her house, sets her table, bids all welcome to her feast. And her feast is Life.

She is the embodiment of God in human life. We seek wisdom, the revelation of God, in our own experience. . . . All one's imagination and discernment may be brought to bear to recognize Wisdom/Sophia. And it takes time, a whole lifetime, to find her.

Today we celebrate the face of Wisdom/Sophia in the lives of the mature women of this community. Women who once would have been given the honored title CRONE in days when grey hair and wrinkles signaled wisdom, power and freedom. Crones were the women whose life-creating monthly blood had ceased to flow. This blood they hold within them now as "wise blood."

Crones were indispensable members of their community . . . They were the healers and midwives of the community, presiders at the moments of great life-transformation: from womb to world, from childhood to adulthood, from sickness to health, from life to death.

The crone's symbol was her kettle, cooking pot, cauldron, itself a symbol of transformation. For nothing that goes into a cooking pot comes out the same! Discrete heaps of carrot, onion, rutabaga, and garlic undergo some magical chemical reaction when a little heat is applied, and become soup. Something happens to the cooks of such a brew also as they create it: from devoted attention to the recipe to the increased freedom and pleasure of following eyes, nose, and taste to create a feast un-imagined by the authors of the cookbook.

The wise women we honor today are retired and working. They come from all sorts of backgrounds. With sixty bells we honor their years.

A MUSICIAN rings bells. WOMEN OVER SIXTY stand while the bells ring.

This wisdom's Feast, brewing in our community kettle, needs your seasoning and stirring, just as this community needs your wisdom.

READER: My child, from your youth choose discipline,
and when you have gray hair you will still find
    wisdom . . .
Search out and seek, and she will become known to you;
and when you get hold of her, do not let her go.
Eccl 6:18, 23-26 (excerpted)

READER: Come to me, all you that are weary and are carrying
heavy burdens, and I will give you rest. . . .
Matt 11:28-29 (excerpted)

Another READER offers the Invocation.

READER: Does Sophia not call?
Does discernment not lift up her voice?
    On the hilltop, on the road,
At the crossroads, she takes her stand;
beside the gates of the city she cries aloud
"O people! I am calling to you!
    My cry goes out to all!
You ignorant ones, study discretion!
    And you fools—come to your senses!
Listen, I have serious things to tell you
    from my lips come honest words.
My children—listen to me!

"Listen to instruction and learn to be wise
    do not ignore it.
Happy those who keep my ways
Happy the one who listens to me
who day after day watches at my gates
to guard the portals.
For the one who finds me finds life . . .
(all who hate me are in love with death.)"[27]
Prov 8:1-6, 32-36

[27] This translation is from *The Jerusalem Bible*, Doubleday & Co., 1966. Sophia, the transliteration of the Greek word for wisdom, is used in place of wisdom.

Come O Holy Sophia, Come!
Fill us with your presence!
Our eyes are open
Our ears are open to receive you
Come!
We honor the years that lead to you
Sixty years that lead to Wisdom
Come!

THE FIRST ACTION: WOMEN GOSSIPING AT THE KITCHEN TABLE

The word "gossip" comprises God and sibbe (cognate sibyl, wise woman).[28]
*Gossip is the wisdom of God revealed in the talk of women. The gossiping is
carried on by THREE WOMEN sitting at a table at one end of the chapel.
The talk is spontaneous, but these questions frame the conversation: What
has life taught you? What has death taught you? What have you had to
"live down"? What has been taken from you? What have you willingly
given up? What don't you worry about anymore? What does it take to
change a life, to transform a world? (Big questions, but they represent the
wisdom of gossiping.)*

*When the women end their conversation, EVERYONE responds with
a chant, sung four times.*

ALL *(chanting four times):*
She changes everything she touches;
everything she touches changes.[29]

*Then begins the remembering of a wide circle of women's wisdom in the form
of a litany. These words and others are called out by DIFFERENT VOICES:*

VOICES *(calling out from different places in the space):*
Gossip, Spinster, Crone, Witch, Maker, Mother, Cook,
Healer, Midwife, Sister, Judge, Prophet, Pilgrim, peace-
maker, Marcella, Claire, Hilda, Julian of Norwich,
Brigid, Mechtilde, Hildegarde, Mother Ann Lee, Anne
Hutchinson, Joan of Arc, Harriet Tubman, Emma
Lazarus, Maria Jesus Alvarada Rivera, Sojourner Truth
. . .

[28] Nor Hall, *The Moon and the Virgin* (New York: Harper & Row, 1980) 189.
[29] Starhawk, *Dreaming the Dark: Magic, Sex, and Politics* (Boston: Beacon
Press, 1982) 226.

THE SECOND ACTION: WITCHES AT THE COOKING POT

This second action incorporates knowledge that cooking is a process of transformation that can lead to different outcomes:

> Water + Herbs + heat = medicine/poison
> Water + Herbs + onions + celery + chicken = soup

In the center of the space, TWO MATURE WOMEN, one stirring fresh herbs into the pot, are talking about a family legend. It is a story about the planting of a tree, a tree that stands as a symbol of the healing of a nation. The CONGREGATION who has moved to this area overhears their conversation.

WOMEN: . . . But what the tree stands for must be planted now, to Inspire, to change things. It should be on the top of the Capitol, or the Kremlin, or the tallest church in the world, or the U.N.—somewhere.

I see, Old one. I see. Let's go!

We are old women; we shall carry it as far as we can. We shall go on entreating, working, nurturing, risk the ridicule, risk the gossip. We've planted trees before.

Suppose we can't make our goal?

Let them there take it up! *(pointing to the congregation).* Out there are the future Old Ones. Let them carry it until all is whole again and the "curse of destruction is abolished."[30]

At the conclusion of this conversation, following an Armenian tradition of storytelling, one WOMAN throws out three apples: one for the TELLER, one for the LISTENER, and one for those who hear the word of God (the CONGREGATION) to remind us that we are all responsible for transforming and abolishing the curse of destruction.
The CONGREGATION responds.

ALL *(chanting four times):*
> She changes everything she touches,
> and everything she touches changes.

---

[30] This story was prepared and told by Eileen Tobin.

The first litany is repeated, but with these and other names added.

VOICES *(calling out from different places in the space):*
Margaret Sanger, Rachel Carson, Katharine Ordway, Mary Mcleod Bethune, Mother Jones, Li Tim Oi, Dorothy Day, Phoebe Howard, Clara Hale, Regina Jonas . . .

THE THIRD ACTION: SPINSTER/CRONE SPINNING
THE THREADS OF HUMAN LIFE

A CRONE tells the story of her life, a succinct version mentioning important insights, turning points, dreams dashed and fulfilled.
   ALL repeat the same chant as before.

ALL *(chanting four times):*
She changes everything she touches,
and everything she touches changes.

Then comes the litany, a repetition with still more new names added.

VOICES *(calling out from different places in the space):*
Miriam, Sophia, Huldah, Deborah, Ruth, Naomi, Anna, Mary, Widow, Dorcas, Theca, women in our lives . . . .

ALL chant a new stanza.

ALL *(chanting):* We are changers. Everything we touch can change.[31]

The rest of the CONGREGATION bless the WOMEN OVER SIXTY.

ALL: Sophia, Crone, female face of God,
We recognize you in the wisdom of the women
      gathered here.
We reverence their years and honor their experience.
Bless them with health, with energy, with courage
To proclaim your presence in the world
      teaching, changing, making all things new.

[31] Ibid.

Then ALL join in singing Ann Patrick Ware's hymn "God, Female God,"[32]
a comforting, joyful song modeled from Brian Wren's hymn "Bring Many
Names."

ALL *(singing):*

> God, female God, working at your loom,
> Weaving strands of life with hands so roughened,
>> getting women toughened;
>> World, beware, make room!
> Hail and Hosanna,
> God, female God!
>
> God, aged crone, stirring iron pot,
> As we sit and gossip 'round your table,
>> Are we really able
>> to reshape our lot?
> Hail and Hosanna,
> God, aged crone!
>
> God, hag and witch, infinitely wise,
> You can be yourself, say what you want to.
>> No one now dare taunt you,
>> Freedom's in your eyes.
> Hail and Hosanna,
> Hag, witch and God!

Then the WOMEN OVER SIXTY bless the CONGREGATION.

WOMEN OVER SIXTY:

> Sophia, Crone, God female God,
> you teach us, stretch us, support us, empower us.
> We feast at your table, eat your bread, and drink
>> your wine.
> We now ask you to bless this community.
> Give them insight, joy, humor,
> patience, anger and gratitude.
> Bless them with long lives

---

[32] The most widely used tune for this hymn is WESTCHASE by Carlton
Young which can be found in the Chalice Hymnal (no. 10), the New Century
Hymnal (no. 11), and Voices United—United Church of Canada Hymnal
(no. 268).

With freedom from regret and guilt.
Bless them with wonder at your marvels.
Bless their experiences broken open with pain
Bless them, Sophia, Crone, God female God.
Bless them. Bless them. Bless them.

CONGREGATION: Amen.

We complete our liturgy by eating the soup that we had watched and smelled and seen transformed throughout our liturgy.

WHY IS THIS LITURGY FEMINIST?

1. God, generally portrayed with male terms, is revealed as Wisdom, in the image of an old woman, wise from the course of life. Rabbi Maggie Wenig, in her own development of a description of God as a woman growing older, argues for this image: "These are the metaphors that enable us to speak of the complex dynamics of relationship: of loyalty and betrayal, love and loss, presence and absence, offense and forgiveness, separation and reunion."[33]

2. Older women, often marginalized in our society, disregarded, forgotten, put away, are here as our teachers, helpers, guides, and healers.

3. Negative images of women—witch, gossip, crone—are given alternative interpretations.

4. No "elite" speaks for all in this liturgy. Many different voices are solicited and heard. Everyone is blessed and offers blessing.

5. Though this liturgy engaged eighty or so people, everyone participated through responses to readings, chants, litanies, and eating soup together.

6. Smells, sights, sounds, movement, mind and body, heart and spirit, were all engaged. There was an appeal to the whole person, not merely the intellect.

7. The planning included people who were experienced and inexperienced, each learning from the other.

8. Elements of contemporary culture were incorporated through new words to old songs.

[33] Margaret Moers Wenig, "Reform Jewish Worship: How Shall We Speak of Torah, Israel, and God" in Procter-Smith and Walton, 42. Wenig's own description of "God Is a Woman and She Is Growing Older" can be found in *Reform Judaism* 21:1 (Fall 1992) 26–28, 44, 45.

9. Ancient texts mixed with new texts. Familiar and perhaps uncomfortable images offered insight to continue the unfolding revelation of a mysterious, unpredictable God.

10. Halloween, a season to remember and imagine saints and sinners, was given a fresh twist.

4 Feminist Liturgy: Applications to Institutional Liturgies

Feminist liturgies, like those included in the preceding section, may seem to some to be "occasional liturgies," that is, conceived, planned, and performed in response to a particular need for one-time use. To understand them primarily as "occasional" misses the point. These examples express a faith that connects with the lived, everyday realities of people whose truths have been neglected, rejected, or distorted in patriarchal religious traditions. The liturgies demonstrate a determination to survive within these traditions or alongside them when institutional authorities have said, "not yet" or "not true" or "only a passing fad." Feminist liturgies signify a refusal to surrender the claim to be Christians or Jews or religious persons. The examples are not ends in themselves, but they are illustrations of a process. They disclose what happens when liturgical planning includes asking, listening, experimenting, and a widening of the circles of traditions.

The urgency and persistence of feminist liturgies are reminiscent of the ways that slave communities in earlier periods of U.S. history dealt with the fact that white men controlled institutional worship.[1] The official prayer of these churches did certainly not contribute to an experience of freedom for black people. Rather it was one more reminder of their oppression, and, in this religious context,

---

[1] See Albert Raboteau, *Slave Religion: The "Invisible Institution" in the Antebellum South* (New York: Oxford University Press, 1986). I first made this connection after reading the Ph.D. dissertation of Scott Haldeman, an extensive historical study of the implications of race and ritual in U.S. Protestantism. I am indebted to him for his work on this subject.

an oppression seemingly sanctioned by God. The story of the Invisible Institution, the performance of faith outside the parameters of established religious churches, testifies that slaves did not buy white people's perspectives nor did they live within their restrictions. Despite the risks, slaves met secretly to do their own rituals. This action, as Melva Costen reminds us, was not an accident of a few rebellious people. Rather "it was a divine necessity":

> The hypocrisy of a distorted gospel, heard under the influence of slave masters who desired to keep slaves in check, forced the slaves to identify what elements would embody the freedom promised by God. Hearing the words of the Bible interpreted in the light of their oppression freed the slave worshipers to pour out their sufferings and needs and express their joys in their own sacred space. Separate and apart from those who denied their freedom on earth, slaves were free in worship to hear and respond to the Word of God.[2]

For gatherings of the Invisible Institution slaves went to their own cabins, brush arbors, and places outdoors; there they prayed and sang and used their bodies to express the depths of their sorrow and the strength of their confidence and joy in the midst of oppression. God was with them, God heard them, no matter what anyone else said or did. They *performed* a vision of freedom. For a few hours, they lived "as if" they were liberated from degradation and dehumanization.[3]

So, too, with feminist liturgies, women and some men, make sacred spaces for ritualizing within homes and outdoors. We listen, speak, sing, and dance our faith through an experience that transforms us. It is an alternative vision for all our relationships. Though the risks and experiences of our ritualizing are quite different from slaves in the Invisible Institution the choice is similar: surrender or survival.[4] Survival demands courage, persistence, and action. Survival

---

[2] Melva Wilson Costen, *African American Christian Worship* (Nashville: Abingdon, 1993) 48–49.

[3] See James Cone's important article, "Sanctification, Liberation and Black Worship" in *Theology Today* 35 (July 1978) 139–52.

[4] Examples abound of people losing job opportunities, being regularly threatened, put down when they participate in public expressions of feminist liturgies or offer interpretations of texts that diverge from traditional or more acceptable explanations. The response to the "Reimagining Conference" in Fall 1996, a gathering of women and some men to re-envision Christian theology and liturgy, in Minneapolis is one example.

includes taking seriously our responsibility for ritualizing, for imagining something different and regularly gathering to enact it.

The purpose of this book is not primarily to laud feminist liturgies for their own sake (though gratitude for them is in order) but rather to make available what has been learned from feminist liturgies so that it can be used, both in institutional settings and, where institutions are not yet ready for feminist input, outside them. To do feminist liturgy is not difficult, but it does require time, intention, skill development, imagination, and boldness.

A. A Planning Process

Some people may know immediately how to apply the material in this book to their liturgies. But, for most people, such changes require a gradual process usually marked by small steps, with an occasional forward leap. To do liturgy described as "feminist" is to try something, something different, that intends to embody what is true for the people involved. At first, the changes may be only a few small adjustments to what has been regularly done at weekly institutional liturgies. Even the smallest changes deepen connections, expand our visions, widen circles of accountability, and enhance our courage to act justly. Every step matters. What follows are two practical applications of this material: a description of a planning process and thoughts for weekly liturgies.

A typical planning process, usually over a three- to four-week period, includes six steps: conversation, pooling ideas and resources, practice, doing the liturgy, evaluation, and going home.

1. Conversation

Feminist liturgies begin with conversation about what is happening in our communities and world, what we're learning about ourselves, what we want to do with our lives, and how belief in God relates to our lives. Conversation helps us to stay in touch with the complexity and certainty of divine relationships and the challenges of human ones. In other words, feminist liturgies start with listening, hearing all kinds of people: grandparents, teenagers, parents, single people, the sorrowing and the joyful, the depressed, the bored, and the hopeful, thereby tuning in to the Spirit/God. Different expressions augment our grasp of the real stuff of life and death, so critical to liturgy.

Talking with varied persons changes what we expect and what we do in our liturgies. Many examples come to mind: a woman coping with a husband in the midst of an affair may need less joyful singing and more texts and sounds that help her to feel her pain and find God with her in the confusion and hurt; a grandmother, like many growing older whose friends all too often die, may want liturgical spaces where it's easy to see her friends, to chat with them before the liturgy begins, to know they are all right; a child wants liturgies to reflect her insights and ideas to be taken seriously as a valuable resource for liturgical experiences.

The list goes on; the point is clear. No one really knows for any other. Though everyone's needs cannot be met directly every time, still asking and listening at the beginning of any planning sets a tone about care and inclusion, with faith intimately connected to every aspect of life. This spirit inevitably finds its way into the liturgies, sometimes concretely, sometimes less visibly.

Conversation leads to more particular planning. If the group begins with a text (the reading assigned by the lectionary or a chosen text) they may begin by studying it, reading it several times, listening for slightly different interpretations from one another and from layers of traditions about the text. Hearing it over and over, with some reflection or silence between the readings, often yields an angle or an insight that becomes a focus of the liturgy. If, on the other hand, the liturgy centers on a particular need, e.g., healing, the blessing of a home, or marking a transition, the conversation may begin with sharing expectations about this ritual, some talking about what the group wants to know and express. For example, in the preparation of a liturgy following the death of a family member, after they have talked about the life and family of the person being remembered, they may discuss the meaning of death, the role it plays in their own relationships, what they want to know about death in this liturgy, and the particular kind of knowing available in ritualizing that happens when all the senses are involved.

In the midst of conversations, there are always hints about a focus for the liturgy. Inevitably resources also emerge, names of people who can help, commentaries that would add information, complementary texts, ideas for music, as well as possibilities for opening the traditional symbols more expansively and for shaping the environment to evoke honesty and beauty.

Decisions follow. Depending on where the community stands along the spectrum of experience, the decisions may range from working on one aspect of the liturgy, for example, the arrangement of space or the language of texts, to planning that is more extensive, such as experimentation with an unfamiliar liturgical form. Conversation that keeps the content of the ritualizing close to the realities and needs of the community is our most reliable way of assuring a reasonable degree of success toward truth-telling.

2. Pooling Ideas and Resources

Often the planning for feminist liturgies occurs over two meetings, one to begin our thinking together and the next to provide development and fine tuning. The period from one meeting to another gives space to sharpen insights, heighten feelings, and add ideas. The goal of a second gathering is to come to consensus about what will be done and to assign responsibilities. For example, where the group has decided to follow a familiar form but to change the arrangement of the space, people may bring for discussion some illustrations of various arrangements along with some anticipated responses to the ramifications of change. Once a decision is made, some will work to carry it out. Or when the group wants to try some changes in the language of texts they may present them for a trial run, in the form of a variety of possibilities from which the group chooses. Planning effective liturgy requires many more ideas than can be used in order to find the most compelling ones. Since feminist liturgies assume imagining, correcting, and doing, such fine tuning is an essential part of doing liturgy responsibly.

3. Practice

Effective ritualizing requires focused interaction between leaders and communities. Practice is critical to the development of habits of attentiveness and responsiveness.

a. The Leaders. Trying out ideas before doing them publicly is necessary. It respects the importance of collaborative liturgical work. Practice works out kinks, smoothes transitions, eliminates excess, opens levels of interpretations, and develops performance skills. Leaders who take the time to practice are less likely to repeat outworn vocal sounds, such as "the preacher's voice" also known as "the holy voice," or present monotonous readings that lack the naturalness of human speech or the feelings connected with their own lives.

With rehearsal, leaders are more likely to discover the multiple meanings in texts, sounds, and spaces and they are more able to lead worship with attentiveness to its power, its integrity, and its beauty. Whether the group is small or large, rehearsal includes going through every detail with all the props in place. Just as many professional actors read their scripts from beginning to end everyday, even though they have long ago committed them to memory and performed them as many as eight times a week, so, too, leaders of communal worship must practice regularly so that they can welcome with confidence whatever happens, planned or unplanned. Good liturgy warrants detailed preparation.

b. The Congregation. Practice is important for the people who gather as well. It heightens anticipation; it ensures familiarity and opens interior spaces so that people can drink ever more deeply and even more spontaneously of the power of liturgy. Groping for words, sounds, a place in a text or in the space diminishes the possibility of relaxed, interactive participation. Practice takes seriously the contribution of each person. Where there is a sense of the coresponsible work of liturgy, communities want to practice. They know its value. It becomes a regular part of the celebration, indeed, one that is enjoyable. When congregations resist rehearsal it is often because they miss the point of their role in helping the liturgical action to happen for themselves and for each other.

4. The Liturgy

Well-prepared and rehearsed, the time comes for the liturgy, eagerly anticipated moments of holiness, beauty, hope, and freedom that the community makes possible by its faith and presence. Liturgical scholar Joseph Gelineau describes the action this way: liturgy involves throwing balls to each other, tossing balls back and forth, each person catching and throwing the ball on her or his own terms. It is not a time for caution, passing on traditions while maintaining control of how they are received. Rather it is a time for risk-taking, tossing what we are giving and receiving as if with a ball. Some of it will be caught, some will not. It depends on how the balls are thrown, whether a person can catch or even wants to catch them.[5]

---

[5] Joseph Gelineau, "The Symbols of Christian Initiation" in *Becoming a Christian Today,* ed. William Reedy (New York: Sadlier, 1979) 194.

At every liturgical action, the community simply embodies an invitation, "come, see, take part, take a chance." The gathering of people makes this invitation available and tangible.

5. Closure

Often the planning process neglects the importance of the ending of worship. Sometimes we think (or hope) it will just happen. But, it doesn't. The ending requires attention. It bridges the power of this liturgy to our everyday lives. How will we remember the power of this liturgy when we need it? How will it matter in the living of our lives? Some words or sounds or movements are needed at the end of a liturgical celebration to connect the holiness of this moment to all our moments. So we plan a succinct expression using words, gestures, sounds, to remind us that this company of friends and this Spirit of God will accompany us wherever we are. We have the power to speak truthfully, to resist injustice, to act with integrity, to notice beauty, to take some chances.

6. Evaluation

To ensure that the tasting and rubbing together of human and divine life seeps into our beings at our liturgies, regular, ongoing evaluation is important. Guessing or presuming is not enough; asking and listening are essential. Evaluation takes different forms but it usually involves questions about what has and has not happened in the liturgy. An evaluation may start with a description of the experience to see what people actually noticed.[6] From these details discussion may move on to more pointed observations including what made our hearts sing or what was boring and unconnected. Evaluation also includes comments about the general overall rhythm of the liturgy and the performance of leaders and participants. What we can learn unfolds bit by bit, over time. Each piece of knowledge becomes a layer of expertise. Occasionally, it is helpful to hear from someone who knows more about public performances, such as an artist or someone who studies liturgy.

---

[6] See Part I, section 2, "Mapping the Field of Ritual" for ideas of a framework in Ronald Grimes, *Beginnings in Ritual Studies* (New York: University Press of America, 1982).

B. Applying the Principles of Feminist Liturgies to Weekly Worship[7]

1. Space

Whether the worship space is new, renovated, or unrenovated, it is a visible and tangible expression of the connections between a community's action inside and outside the building. The space itself is a witness of faith and it evokes a dynamic witness in us. It constantly stirs up faith disturbed by injustice and therefore committed to right it. The space itself expresses a community's commitment to the neighborhood and to the world community to be in solidarity with the economic, social, environmental struggles that press all people into action. Inside the space is arranged so that people notice each other; a variety of arrangements, if possible, to accent different expressions of relationships and varied expressions of common quests. These friends and strangers from all sorts of backgrounds and with all types of abilities are the faces of God or as David Power states it, "the traces of God," among us.

The space invites our looking, seeing, hearing, touching, talking with one another. It sets a tone of collective responsibility to remake the space as "sacred" every time we gather, to claim solidarity with

[7] Some reliable resources for application of feminist principles and additional bibliography: Tom F. Driver, *Liberating Rites: Understanding the Transformative Power of Ritual* (Boulder, Co.: Westview Press, 1998); Miriam Therese Winter's books, songs, and feminist readings of biblical literature such as *WomanWord, WomenWisdom,* and *WomanWitness* (New York: Crossroad); Marcia Falk, *The Book of Blessings* (San Francisco: HarperSanFrancisco, 1996); Marjorie Procter-Smith and Janet Roland Walton, eds. *Women at Worship* (Louisville: Westminster/John Knox Press, 1993); Ada Maria Isasi-Diaz, *Mujerista Theology* (Maryknoll, N.Y.: Orbis Books, 1996); The Re-Imagining Community, *Bring the Feast* (Cleveland: Pilgrim Press, 1998); Marjorie Procter-Smith, *Praying with Our Eyes Open* (Nashville: Abingdon Press, 1995); Gail Ramshaw, *Liturgical Language* (Collegeville: The Liturgical Press, 1996); Ruth Duck, *Finding Words for Worship: a Guide for Leaders* (Louisville: Westminster/John Knox Press, 1995); Kittredge Cherry and Zalmon Sherwood, eds., *Equal Rites: Lesbian and Gay Worship, Ceremonies, and Celebrations* (Louisville: Westminster/John Knox Press, 1995); Priests for Equality, *The Inclusive New Testament* (Brentwood: Priests for Equality, 1994); Lesley A. Northup, *Ritualizing Women* (Cleveland, Oh.: The Pilgrim Press, 1997); Diann L. Neu and Mary E. Hunt, *Women-Church Sourcebook* (Washington, D.C.: WATERworks, 1993).

one another, an interdependent spirit where every person urges another to know again the promises of God. The space through its designs, colors, textures, proportions, and scale remind us that dreams, fears, horrors, joys, despair are the stuff of freedom. They have a place here. Even the least addition or change in the space makes a difference. Sacred space takes every aspect of the person seriously, regardless.

2. The Gathering of the People

This day is eagerly awaited, it is the time to reconstitute themselves as a liturgical community. Ordained and lay, professional and amateur, this community reflects a curious mix of gender, races, economic background, physical appearance (e.g., fat, thin, well and ill, in wheel chairs, able to walk), age, maturity, and experience. Children mill around with pride, finding spaces set up with activities in which they can be involved. Adolescents claim their particular roles, interpretive tasks through sound, art, movement, and words. The time begins with catching up, conversation with each other about what has happened since the last time this community has gathered. For those who want some quiet, reflective time there is a small space set up for them.

3. The Liturgy Begins

A member of the congregation invites everyone gathered to welcome one another and especially anyone who is a guest. She gives an update about the community, with limited announcements, only the news best shared person to person. Someone with community building skills follows, maybe a musician or a juggler or a dancer. Since liturgical action addresses body, mind, heart, and soul all at once, we wake up and warm up all our senses to be ready.

4. Prayer

Needing the Spirit of God and every other venue of relationship for our liturgical work, we intentionally and expectantly call upon God and all saints, living and dead, to be present. At times we remember particular people by name, sources of encouragement and strength. We call upon God through an endless array of images, whatever is appropriate to the time and our needs. Our liturgical action requires, in Elizabeth Johnson's words, "an intergenerational company of persons profoundly touched by the sacred, sharing in the cosmic community of life which is also sacred"[8] to stand with us.

Though we are aware that the whole liturgical action is prayer we give time for particular kinds of prayer at various times throughout the liturgy. In addition to strengthening ourselves with the company of those not visible to us, we spend time listening to one another express immediate concerns, from family, neighborhood, and world. And we have silent prayer for whatever connections we want to make, for whatever emotions we feel. Not token moments, but enough time to allow the flow of prayer, its rhythms of intensity and rest.

5. Readings, Music, and Action

Somewhere in the time for worship we remember stories of freedom and hope, God and humans and the created world in actions that lead to redemption. We recall myths from classical sacred literature and contemporary resources. Sometimes they are read, sometimes sung, danced, visualized. What is most important is that these stories are told over and over and over, so that they become layered in us, resources to call upon as we need them.

Music accompanies us on our way. We use songs and instrumental music to respond to what we've heard or seen, and to add interpretations to the stories that focus our lives. Music provides our bodies with active ways to reinforce what we are doing together, on a journey with each other to claim freedom for ourselves and for one another, near and far. We sing all kinds of songs, treasured hymns and new ones, music from a variety of cultures and contemporary music, too. We use drums, accordions, saxophones, harmonicas as well as guitars, clarinets, organs, harps, and pianos. Every sound provides a distinctive lens, a particular expression of human emotion and perception. We need them all to accent and extend and enhance our imagination, and our courage.

Our liturgical work is to make connections, within ourselves and beyond ourselves, connections that express God's commitment and ours. Our liturgical work is to learn how to rely on the strength of the experience beyond this time and space. When we are called upon to step up, to take a stand on behalf of one another in the local

[8] Elizabeth Johnson, *Friends of God and Prophets: A Feminist Theological Reading of the Communion of Saints* (New York: Continuum, 1998) 2.

or global community, to live into our faith, our connections can steady us and urge us and stand by us. Imperfect and incomplete we nevertheless continue to eat, listen, talk, walk, sing, anoint, bless, as if what is possible is realized, if only for these moments. Our human actions reflect divine priorities that no one goes hungry, that abuse is never permissible, that every person deserves justice and dignity. This sacred space requires an extension to all space, to make it sacred, too. As James Baldwin says: "People pay for what they do, and even more, for what they have allowed themselves to become. And they pay for it simply: by the lives they lead."[9]

6. The Arts

Visual, kinetic, verbal, and gestural art are important to our liturgical work. Liturgies rely on a variety of languages to express meanings, meanings that are disclosed bit by bit, layer by layer, as stories are told and heard, as things are seen and tasted, as people are touched. Liturgical communities require many avenues of access to these meanings. Some of us see more easily than we hear; some of us understand through the movement of our bodies more readily than listening to words; some of us need to touch what is conveyed before we grasp what is being presented to us. Art provides varied possibilities for our perception and participation. Art also intends to express beauty and truth, not facts, but the experience of what is beyond us and in us and around us.

Art attempts to connect what we do not know with what we are yearning to know. It presumes sacred, interactive spaces where persons can respond from the distinctiveness of their own experiences to what is encountered. The arts are not meant to lay out meanings but are intended to echo them back, like a boomerang. They work best when there is space in the liturgy for interaction. Some examples include a temporary art exhibit in the vestibule of the church or synagogue, an image on the screen during the liturgy, a story told through movement, young people rapping the scripture to connect life with faith.

7. An End

There is much to do outside this time and space. This liturgy is only a beginning. Here we have heard and tasted a way of living

[9] James Baldwin, *Nobody Knows My Name* (New York: Dial Press, 1961).

where no one is hungry, hurt or despised. Though it is difficult we go to do likewise. The insights, wisdom, and beauty of these moments provide courage and new patterns of interaction. God is blessed and we are blessed. A member of the community focuses this power. We go out together sustained and encouraged until the next time.

As in the beginning there is time now for conversation and food for everyone to share. Occasionally this time may also be used to talk about the quality of worship experiences.

The Invisible Institution changed dramatically what blacks expected of themselves, of God, and their world. When they recognized that what whites imposed as the right liturgy for everyone was not right for them, they did something else. Their hunches were confirmed. In these gatherings they felt the freedom promised by God. What they learned they now pass on as a precious resource for all churches.

Similarly, with feminist liturgies. Something quite incredible is happening. People are gathering to develop liturgies that embody freedom and truth-telling in this time of discrimination, when a norm for worship persists tenaciously that limits many people's participation, especially all those marginalized. For almost thirty years feminist liturgies have been planned and celebrated. What we have discovered are also rich resources for churches and synagogues.

"Feminist liturgy? It's not what I thought," says Uncle Clarence. "It's obviously not primarily about 'genderizing the liturgy.' But, I am still quite uneasy. Will all that I have loved and enjoyed have to change?"

Fear of losing what is familiar is a warranted concern. Though feminist liturgies develop from traditions and use traditions, they also correct and add to traditions. Change is inevitable. But, it does not mean eliminating all that is familiar, all well-loved language for God, all scripture texts, all typical forms of preaching, all eucharistic formulas, all comfortable and beautiful spaces. It does require examining them and giving up whatever hurts, hides, or dishonors. Decisions about what should be changed in any community emerge from within each group, the result of the collective processes of reflection, ritualizing and evaluation. The goals are truth-telling, connecting worship of God with justice, that is, liturgies where all people, street dwellers and housed, unemployed and those with jobs, depressed and peaceful, women and children as well as men, people of all races and backgrounds, where all persons can hear, see, believe and evoke the Spirit's power in each other. Such transforming experiences of justice and beauty, the essence of holiness, this is the hope and bequest of feminist liturgies.